pure PLASTIC

New Materials for Today's Architecture

Imprint
The Deutsche Bibliothek is registering this publication in the
Deutsche Nationalbibliographie; detailed bibliographical infor-
mation can be found on the internet at http://dnb.ddb.de

ISBN 978-3-938780-51-0

© 2008 by Verlagshaus Braun
www.verlagshaus-braun.de

1st edition 2008

Editorial staff:
Sophie Steybe, Chris van Uffelen
Draft texts by the architects. Text editing: Chris van Uffelen
Translation:
Alice Bayandin
Graphic concept:
Michaela Prinz
Layout:
Georgia van Uffelen

All of the information in this volume has been compiled to
the best of the editors knowledge. It is based on the information provided to the publisher by the architects' and designers' offices and excludes any liability. The publisher assumes
no responsibility for its accuracy or completeness as well as
copyright discrepancies and refers to the specified sources
(architects and designers offices). All rights to the photographs
are property of the photographer (please refer to the picture
credits).

pure PLASTIC

New Materials for Today's Architecture

BRAUN

Fantastic plastic

In the course of the last century plastics have become an essential component of our culture. In 1984 production of plastic surpassed that of steel for the first time. While only 10,000 tons of plastic were produced worldwide in 1934, in 1949 that number reached 1,000,000 and in 2006, 205,000,000 tons were manufactured.

Architecture can no longer be imagined without plastic – floor coating, wall paper, dome lights, façade elements, fittings, profiles, warmth insulators, foams, laminates, varnishes and glues, and especially cable insulations, PVC pipes and plastic doors and window frames (albeit the latter often come under quite justified criticism) have all become important elements of modern architecture.

The word "plastic" is derived from the Greek "plastikos" which means "to mold or form", and refers to the material's readiness to assume new shape. Plastics are synthetic or semisynthetic long molecule chains (polymers) with organic groups. Semisynthetic plastics like celluloid are created by modification of natural polymers. The intricate polymer chains consist of endlessly repeating basic units, monomers. Naphta, a petroleum distillate, is often used as the starting material that provides short carbohydrate chains.

Variations in the manufacturing process and different additives result in plastics with an extremely wide range of properties. Thermal remolding, hardness and elasticity are just some of the properties that can be influenced directly. Plastics are ordered into three groups according to their properties. Thermoplastics can be reversibly shaped under the influence of heat (plastic bags, celluloid). In contrast, thermosetting plastics are shaped only once, but thanks to their tight molecule nets can withstand great temperatures without losing their form (pot handles and artificial resins). Finally, elastomers are flexible due to their loose molecule netting (rubber bands).

The search for a moldable, hard-setting and durable material is almost as old as the history of man. In the Neolithic period humans mixed mammoth fir and clay to create "plastic". Resin, amber, rubber and wax are natural materials that resemble plastic. In the 15th century, paper-maché technique was developed, followed by an artificial resin made out of goat cheese that was used for wood inlays in the 16th century. The Baroque scagliola technique created a moldable artificial marble or "marmorino", which today could have been perfectly replaced by a plastic.

Exploration of the properties of natural rubber, which was industrially used in the 1820s to rubberize raincoats, greatly expedited the development of plastics. Rubber vulcanization (1839, Charles Goodyear) and production of linoleum using linseed oil also coincided with the announcement of the discovery of the first semisynthetic plastic at the 1862 Great International Exhibition in London. Alexander Parkes discovered Parkesine by mixing chloroform and castor oil, and his work introduced the idea of giant molecules (1861/63). The "poly" (greek: many) from the word polymer is found in most names and abbreviations of plastic types. Parkes' discovery, whose chemical makeup resembled that of an explosive, was meant to replace ivory... and produce bouncing billiard balls. In 1907, Leo Henry Baekeland took out the patent for the first completely synthetic plastic,

Bakelite. This plastic was a thermoset isolation material that was to replace shellac, a natural resin made from plant-sucking insect secretions. Bakelite was extremely prominent in the years between the world wars, but eventually yielded to newer, less brittle materials.

The manufacturing process for PVC was patented in 1912, and polyethylene, used for garbage bags, followed in 1933. In 1935 polyamide, the first completely synthetic fiber that is much wider known as nylon began to define the eroticism of the post-war years – even the music of this time was played back from vinyl, not shellac.

The material that was marketed for the space age nineteen years before Sputnik's flight, polytetrafluorethylene, or PTFE ("Teflon"), was discovered in 1939. One after the other, this age produced the materials that continue to influence our lives to this day – polyester (textile fibers) in 1941, styrofoam (packaging) in 1949, and polycarbonate (CDs) in 1953. Aromatic polyamides that are used in production of high-strength aramid fibers and foils (tennis racquet strings) were discovered in 1965.

Perhaps even more important than pure plastics, are hybrid materials composed of different plastics or only partially of plastics. Thanks to acrylic, laminated glass is splitter-free since 1927. PTFE has been used to produce air-permeable, water-resistant membranes (Goretex) since 1969, and glass-reinforced plastic (GRP) has revolutionized air travel and yacht construction in 1953. Carbon fiber-reinforced plastic is used in vehicle manufacture in some luxury car lines (Porsche Carrera GT). Wood plastic composite (WPC) made using sawdust and recycled PVC and polyethylene produces water-resistant wood which can be used for foundations in moist ground or underwater without rotting.

From the start, plastic was a material that was both celebrated and controversial in its use in architecture. Designers of applied arts saw danger in industrial fabrication, and recognized plastic as a substitute for poor imitation of form. Hermann Muthesius of the German Work Federation (Deutscher Werkbund) held this view.

In contrast, progressive designers like Walther Gropius of Bauhaus saw industry as a partner in proliferation of beautiful forms, and were receptive to the new material. High-pressure laminates like Resopal replaced conventional enamel plates in the 1930s, ensuring uniform surfaces. Bakelite casts enabled mass production, letting Marlene Dietrich's voice be heard from "people's radio" receivers. The emblematic GDR automobile Trabant, manufactured in 3.1 million copies starting in 1957, was stamped out using a proletarian version of GRP made by drowning cotton in phenol resin. In the years following, plastic experienced its breakthrough in product design: in the works of César, Arman and Claes Oldenburg during the pop years as art; as Lego sets, Tupperware and Panton chairs (1960) as mass produced objects.

Plastic's success as a dominating architectural material, however, remained marginal. Examples include Disney's Monosanto House of the Future, made completely out of glass fiber-reinforced polyester (1957) and spurned by the masses, and Matti Suuronen's Futuro, which was discontinued due to the 1973 oil crisis. Overall, proposals and prototypes like Hans Hollein's Mobile Office and Archigram's Control and Choice, dominated the scene.

However, in stadium and hall construction, especially in air-inflated tents like the Metrodome in Minneapolis, plastics were readily employed. In the Olympia Park built for the 1972 Olympics in Munich, membranes and acrylic plates were used, while sanitary units in the Olympic Village were built using large cast components. Out of the 12 arenas used in the 2006 World Cup, nine had plastic roofing. The Allianz Arena deserves a special mention due to its renowned plastic pillows. Step by step, the material is finding its way into noteworthy architecture due to its aesthetic and functional adaptability and expressiveness. This plurality of plastic is illustrated by the examples presented in this book.

Chris van Uffelen

POLYGONAL

01

Fukusaki Hanging Garden, 2005
Address: Fukusaki, Japan. **Structural engineers:**
Kajima Design. **Client:** private. **Materials:** steel sheets,
iron grid, polyvinyl chloride (PVC, "vinyl").

Weak hearts

ARCHITECTS: Kengo Kuma & Associates

The hanging garden is a temporary facility providing space for events and assemblies for children, and is to be taken down and moved after ten years. It is a product of Kengo Kuma's search for "weakness" in the structure and outer walls that are to replace the conventional "strong" structure and "strong" walls. The framework is a grid slab structure considering of two 9 mm-thick steel sheets sandwiching a 50 mm-thin iron grid clamped tight with high-tension bolts to make an ultra-thin slab with a total 68 mm thickness. Ten years from now, the structure can be taken apart to pieces by simply unscrewing the bolts. External walls are made of a soft, thin material known as vinyl curtain. These walls are reinforced with bolts and wires so they can withstand typhoons. The basic idea was that a free space surrounded by "weak" things would liberate the children's hearts and thoughts.

02

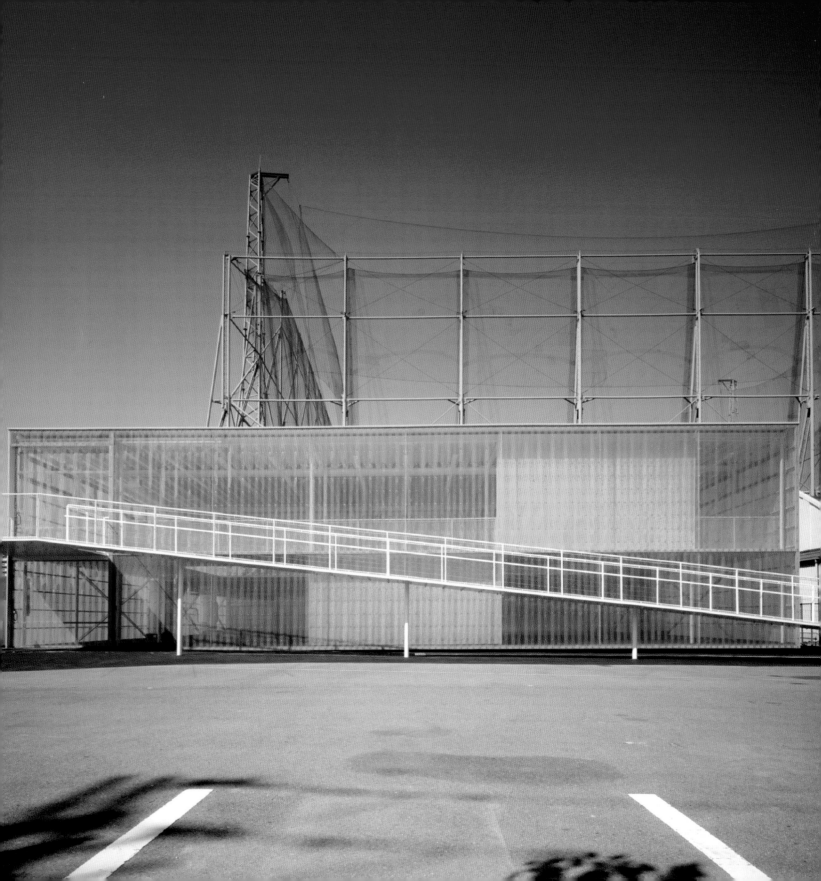

04

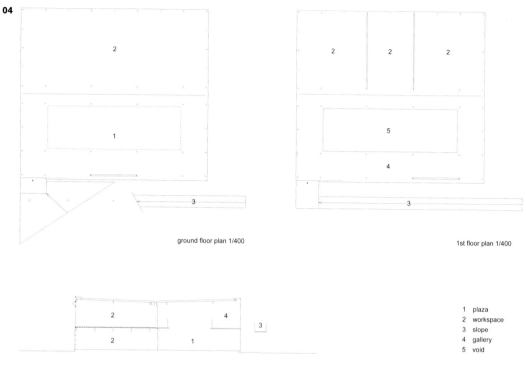

ground floor plan 1/400

1st floor plan 1/400

section 1/400

1 plaza
2 workspace
3 slope
4 gallery
5 void

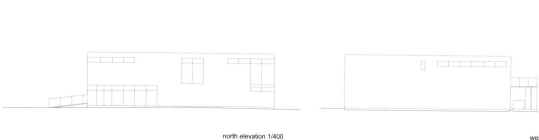

south elevation 1/400

eas

north elevation 1/400

wes

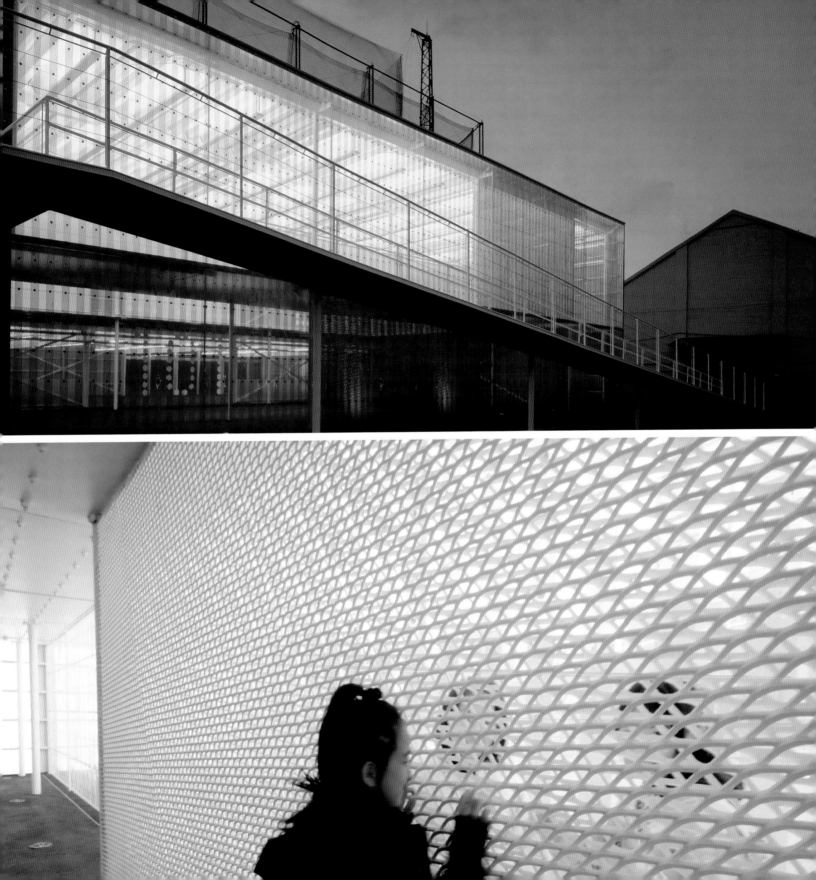

Blur Business Hotel and Cultural Facility, 2006
Address: No.16 DongHuamen Street, Dongcheng
District, Beijing, China. **Project designer:** Pei Zhu,
Tong Wu. **Project team:** Li Chuen, Zhang Pengpeng,
Zhou Lijun, Dai Lili, Wang Min. **Engineers:** Beijing
Zhongjian Hengji Gongcheng Co. Ltd. **Client:** China
Resource. **Gross floor area:** 10,176 m². **Structure and
materials:** reinforced concrete frame (existing struc-
ture), walls made of fiber-reinforced polymer (FRP,
fiber-reinforced plastic)

Plastic bondage
ARCHITECTS: Studio Pei-Zhu

The Blur Hotel, located on the site of a large government
office beside the western Gate of the Forbidden City, is
an experiment in "urban acupuncture". The project aims
to harmonize the existing building with its surroundings
and provide a beacon for renewal of the surrounding
area. The first strategy is to open out the ground floor
to create a layer of traversable space occupied by pub-
lic-oriented programs. The next approach integrates the
building more with the local building typology, the courtyard house. By carving into concrete slab floors, an arrangement of alternating courtyards is created, which
replicates the spatial arrangement of the surrounding
hutongs. The third tactic wraps the exterior in a continuous and semi-transparent façade. The façade material is
FRP, a thermosetting plastic which is translucent, rigid
and corrosion-resistant. Functionally it is used as a protective surface against sunlight. On a conceptual level,
the extraordinary color and texture of FRP created an
image of Chinese boulders, generating a translucent and
glowing effect reminiscent of Chinese lanterns.

01 Exterior view **02** Façade **03** Material detail **04** Section **05** Vertical courtyards **06** Courtyard

04

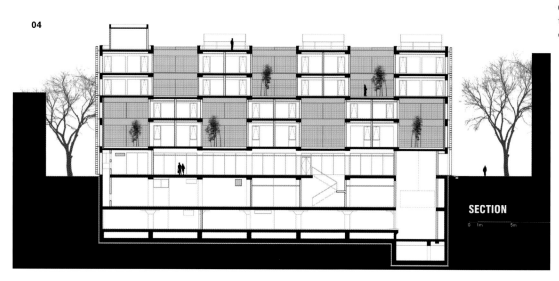

SECTION

0 1m 5m

05

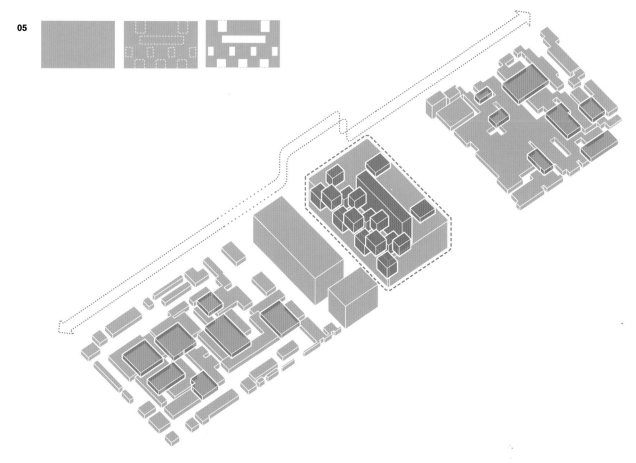

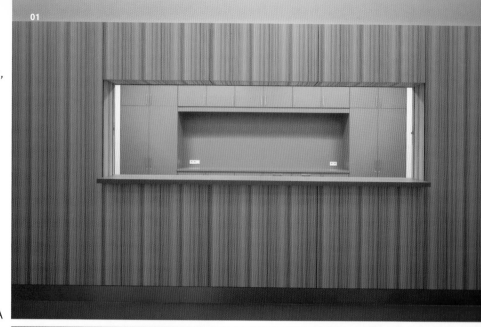

Classroom center Freie Universität Berlin, cafeteria II, 2006
Address: Otto-von-Simson-Straße 26, 14195 Berlin, Germany. **Client:** Freie Universität Berlin, Technische Abteilung. **Gross floor area:** 1,000 m². **Materials:** plaster acoustic ceiling panels, colored, artificial resin seamless floor coating, plaster panels with paint coat, corridor wall cladding, varnished wood, panels made of resopal high pressure laminates (HPL, coated wood panels, "laminate").

A better figure in stripes

ARCHITECTS: Carola Schäfers Architekten BDA

The conference center is characterized by the material and color concept which stresses the originality of the building while newly reinterpreting it. The floor's particularly seamless artificial resin coat emphasizes the special character of the rooms while bringing it together as one entity. The lecture room found inside has been made primarily into an object by using rounded-off corners facing the corridor and wall casing with digitally printed Resopal panels. The encircling, indirect lighting, together with the colorful stripe panels contribute to the impression of the room as an object.

01 Tea kitchen 02 Detail wall 03 Corridor between the classrooms 04 Floor plan 05 Section 06 View into classroom 3 07 Doors classroom 3

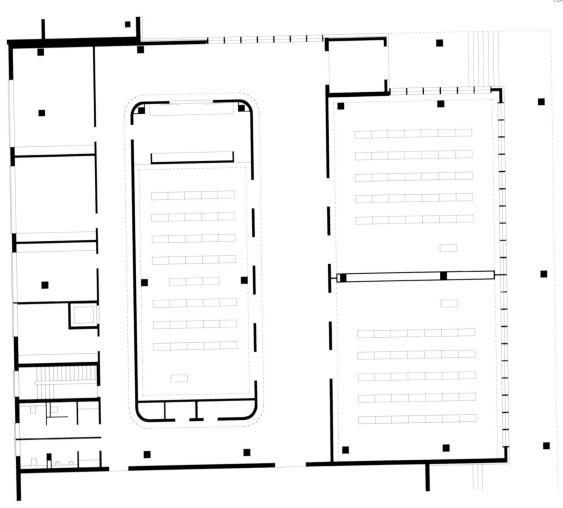

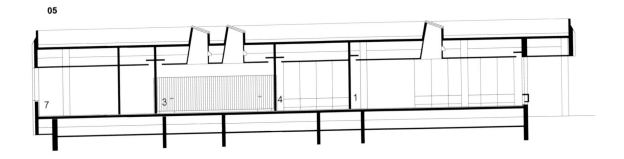

01

Head office enlargement Ilti Luce, 2002
Address: Via Pacini, Torino, Italy. **Client:** Ilti Luce.
Gross floor area: 400 m². **Materials:** steel, reinforced
concrete, brick, aluminum, glass, sheets made of polymethyl methacrylate (PMMA, "acrylic glass").

Artificial horizon
ARCHITECTS: UdA

An additional story covering about 400 m² was built on
top of a flat roof of an existing office block for a company operating in the field of optical fibers for lighting pur-
poses and advanced technology for artificial light. The
additional story stands like a separate body on the existing building and continues independently towards the
inner courtyard. The outer walls were paneled according
to the ventilated façade method with a mosaic-like work
made up of nearly 250 opalescent Methacrylate sheets
fastened to an underlying aluminum frame, covering all
surfaces except for the glass walls at either end. The
framework allows for new technological functions to be
incorporated. It can act as a sun collector for the air in
the cavity between the Methacrylate sheets and the in-
sulating boards, which is then tapped and channeled to
the building interior; or it can host photovoltaic cells to
supply energy to the LED lighting system of the façade.
The aim was above all to turn technology itself into real
matter thanks to the interaction between natural and
artificial light.

02

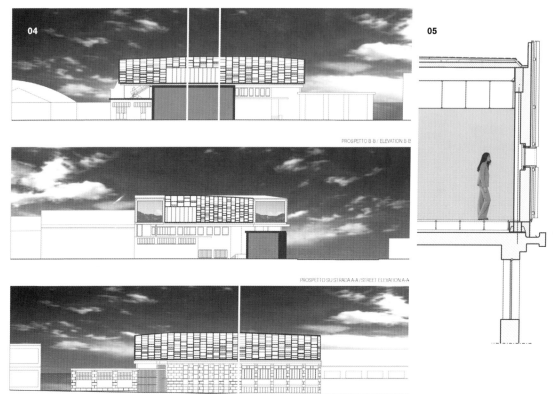

04

PROSPETTO B-B / ELEVATION B-B

PROSPETTO SU STRADA A-A / STREET ELEVATION A-A

05

01 Exterior view **02** Detail material **03** Detail façade **04** Elevations **05** Detail construction **06** General plan **07** Façade seen from the first floor **08** Exterior view

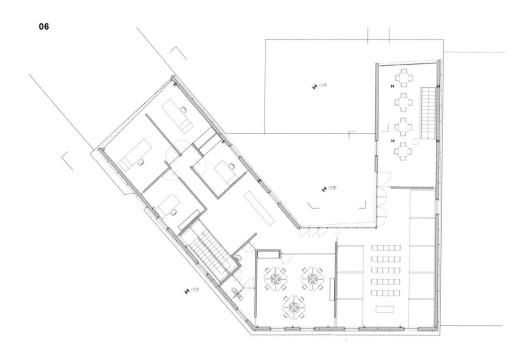

06

Casa GA, 2005
Address: Privada Santa Claudia No. 5835, Tijuana BC, Mexico. **Client:** GA family. **Gross floor area:** 525 m².
Materials: steel structure, galvanized steel, concrete, redwood siding, white polycarbonate (PC).

Twin skins

ARCHITECTS: graciastudio

The plot located on a cliff plunges down on the side of the garden, a characteristic used to create a generous Zen garden that stretches all the way underneath the building. At this point, the building is completely glazed and reveals the steel frame to the eye. The house above is divided into two volumes of approximately equal size, which flank the small tower housing the stairwell. Above the street level the house is clad in metal. The bottom-most story, the walls enclosing the garden and those of one of the main volumes are made of concrete. Most of the rest of the main volume had a wooden façade, which resurfaces in other sections of the main building. This building itself is for the most part encased in polycarbonate corrugates panels. The spectrum of architectonic materials present on the façade is repeated inside, even in the integrated furniture pieces.

04

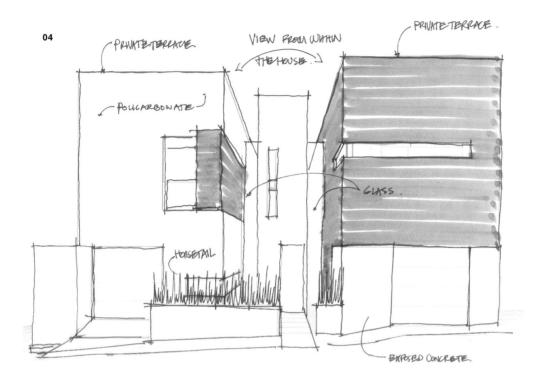

PRIVATE TERRACE

VIEW FROM WITHIN THE HOUSE.

PRIVATE TERRACE.

POLICARBONATE

GLASS.

HORSETAIL

EXPOSED CONCRETE

05

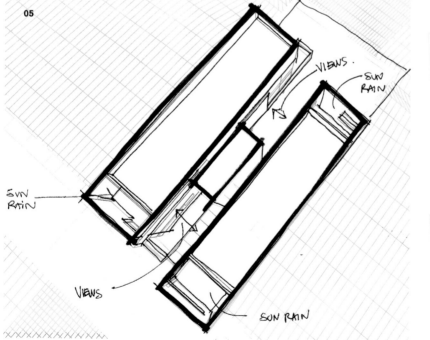

VIEWS.

SUN RAIN

SUN RAIN

VIEWS

SUN RAIN

06

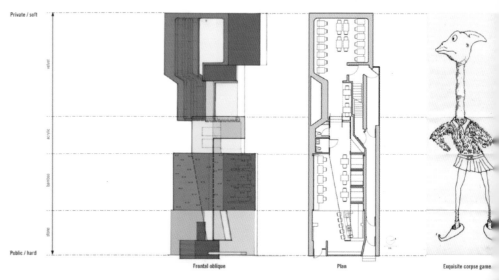

Frontal oblique   Plan   Exquisite corpse game

Xing Restaurant, 2005
Address: 785 9th Avenue, New York, NY 10019, USA.
Client: MiJo: Chow Down Inc. and Michael Lagudis.
Gross floor area: 185 m². **Materials:** velvet, bamboo,
stone, polymethyl methacrylate (PMMA, "acrylic
glass").

Zoning / Bracket
ARCHITECTS: LTL Architects

This Pan-Asian restaurant occupies a floor plan with a
dog-bone-like shape, typical of New York City residential buildings. Rather than hiding this distinctive narrow
section, which is a result of light wells, Lewis.Tsurumaki.
Lewis accentuated the unique nature of each of the
spaces. Following the logic derived from the Surrealists'
game of "Exquisite Corpse", four spaces were composed
as distinct, yet interlocked areas. Each of these areas is
defined by and encased in different materials, progress-
ing in texture from hard at the most public area near the
street entrance, to soft in the most private room. Layered
stone marks the front bar area. Beyond that, an envelope
of bamboo strips defines the booths of the semi-public
seating area. The next zone is a narrow corridor containing the bathrooms and a wait station. The enclosing walls,
steps, and ceiling of this corridor are lined with strips of
vertically stacked colored acrylic held in a steel frame.
This layered acrylic ceiling becomes a tapered extension
over the front dining room where it serves as a light can-
opy before dropping down to become the surface of the
bar. The private dining is enveloped by red velvet panels.

01 Diagram **02** Storefront **03** View from private dining to bar area

Wood materials engineering laboratories, annex building, 2004
Address: School of Architecture and Construction Management, Washington State University, USA.
Sponsoring: US Navy. **Gross floor area:** 501 m².
Materials: wood plastic composite (WPC).

tREe-engineering

ARCHITECTS: Robert Barnstone

The building is an interaction between aesthetic interests and inventive material exploration. It experiments with the potentials of wood plastic composite (WPC), materials that use ultraviolet (UV) light inhibitors and color additives to WPC blends, as well as unique profiles for envelope and rain-screen applications. The building is the result of work by a multidisciplinary team of students and professors with architecture, materials science, and structural engineering backgrounds. The structure is fabricated from complex box beams made entirely from engineered wood products. Frank Lloyd Wright's use of box beams in his later Usonian homes was the inspiration due to their ability to achieve a long span with a minimum of material. Students were asked to design unique box beams for one bay. WPC can be more durable than traditional wood products. It can be extruded to virtually any desired length and molded to a range of shapes. It has no predetermined color or form; it could be made as animated as desired for the building structure.

08

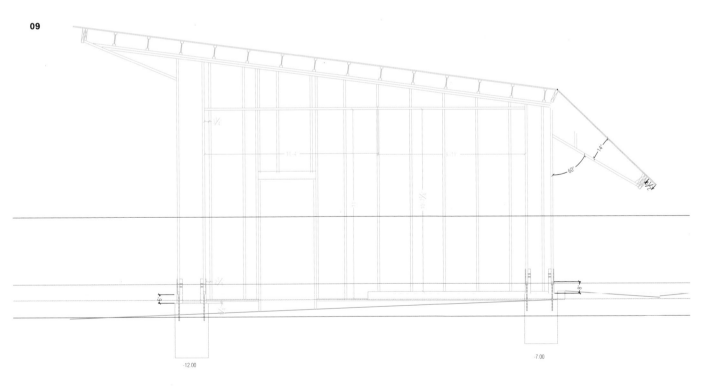

09

Loft in PLUS5, 2005
Address: Technoparkstrasse 6, 8005 Zurich, Switzerland. **Client:** Willy Klossner and Stephan Willi.
Gross floor area: 100 m². **Materials:** concrete, wood, plasterboard wall, polymethyl methacrylate (PMMA, "acrylic glass").

Translucent privacy

ARCHITECTS: Daniele Claudio Taddei Architect

The loft is situated in the Plus5 building complex, which was developed around an historical ship turbine production hall in Zurich. The design tries to emphasize the loft's wide open feel down to the smallest detail. In order to be true to this design concept even in the bathroom, a special refinement in execution was demanded. The wall was built as a metal structure, and a backlit translucent Plexiglas layer was raised in front of the sink, toilet, shower and bathtub. Plexiglas sheets fulfill concept and client requirements: the material is translucent, hermetic, hygienic, clean, elastic, visually appealing, modern, easy to install and affordable. The kitchen, designed as a "social" table in the middle of the space, also follows the concept of openness. This is further emphasized even through the access, a descent from the main entry on the higher level. The different zones of the open loft can be divided by a mobile wall, making its use more flexible.

01 Loft inside the building Plus5 **02** Detail acrylic glass **03** Bathroom **04** Detail bathroom

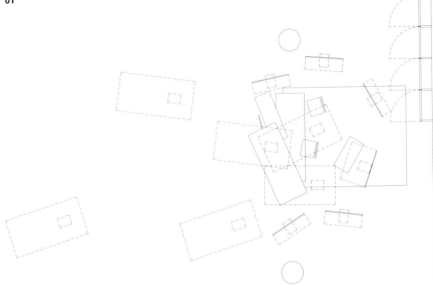

Administrative Building BB Center reception, 1999
Address: BB Center, Praha 4, Czech Republic. **Client:** PSJ INVEST + PASSER INVEST. **Gross floor area:** 10 m², controling the entrance hall of 120 m². **Materials:** Perspex polymethyl methacrylate (PMMA, "acrylic glass").

Who is afraid of ...

ARCHITECTS: Ivan Kroupa architekti

The dried-out space of the entrance hall of a big administrative building is governed by opaque colored sheets in red, yellow and blue that emerge from its nucleus. The system of panel fills up the space with diffused light and defines the reception area consistently. An effect applying geometric principles to organic matter, technology and service is concentrated in the nucleus. The variously colored sheets of Perspex form the basis of this interior. They are reinforced with strips of the same material and subtle metal elements that enable their overlapped hanging. All the sheets levitate without touching the floor or ceiling at all, and each one of them has its own source of light. The ability of the material to transmit, reflect and emit light brings about diffuse colored illumination. The back-and-forth glints, reflections of surrounding architecture and pulsating activity outside and inside of the hall create lively, ever-changing compact matter. Similarly to hard-edge paintings of Barnett Newman, the color surfaces are separated from each other but still reciprocate influencing others.

01 Plan **02** Reception **03 + 04** Detail **05** Foyer with reception

02

05

01

**Parts House Open-Air Entertainment Pavilion, 2004
Address:** 215 West Maple Street, Milwaukee, Wisconsin, USA. **Client:** Joe and Cindy Rewolinski. **Gross floor area:** 140 m². **Materials:** IPÊ wood, sheets made of polymethyl methacrylate (PMMA, "acrylic glass").

Movable mosaik

ARCHITECTS: Johnsen Schmaling Architects

The program required an outdoor living room for intimate dinners and large social events. The space should provide opportunities for seclusion, sunbathing as well as sun and wind protection without compromising the stunning views from the blacktop roof above the client's loft. A pavilion of steel modules supporting a curtain of sliding steel frames sheathed with polychromatic transparent and translucent plastic was designed. Acrylite was used because of its lightweight, weather-resistant qualities, UV ray filtering, shatter-resistance and endless possible color choices. Slip joints and neoprene fasteners compensate for the plastic's expansion and contraction. Depending on their arrangement, the panels provide various levels of privacy or exposure, offer shelter, and act as frame and filter, providing offset views of the city. At night, a sophisticated lighting system transforms them into a highly visible phantasmagoria of colors and shadows. The roof pavilion has become a neighborhood beacon, an extraordinary public spectacle and a symbol of urban vitality. It exemplifies how a small-scale urban intervention can have a major impact on its larger-scale environment.

02

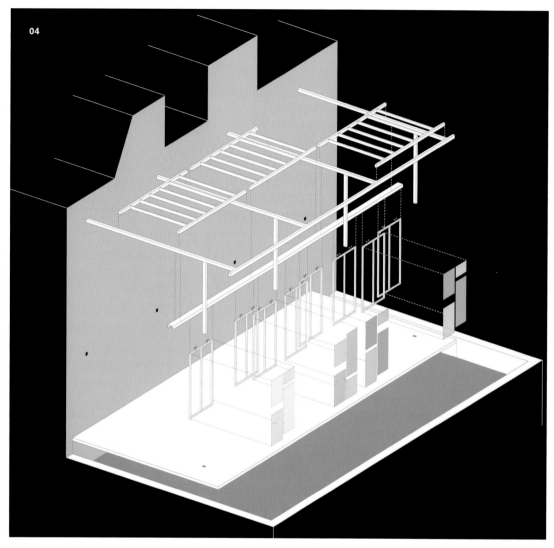

04

01 Night entertainment in pavilion
02 Daylight reflections **03** Nightly
color projections **04** Axonometric
drawing of principal components
05 Conceptual montage: strips of
color organize Milwaukee's som-
ber skyline **06** View of pavilion
with illuminated curtain of plastic
panels

05

Art and Culture House Brasilea, 2005
Address: Basel, Switzerland. **Design:** Arthur Fischer.
Client: Stiftung Brasilea. **Gross floor area:** 1,765 m².
Materials: steel, concrete, corrugate sheets made of
glass-reinforced plastic (GRP).

Brazilian emerald
ARCHITECTS: Fischer Art

A former Rhine shipbuilders' repair shop has been lifted
from its former context without denouncing its origins
through the use of green corrugate sheets made of
glass-reinforced plastic. While the industrial building
is visible behind the translucent material, which re-
introduces the industrial theme into the complex, the
intense color scheme and dynamic light reflections on
the façade clearly separate the cultural center from the
surrounding port structures. The optically low-key reinforced concrete used in the building's base accents the
independence of the new building envelope, which was
placed on top of the raised and fully developed base like
a dress. The previously closed-off façade facing land
is covered with fiberglass completely, while the large
windows facing the river are made even more appar-
ent. Due to this, the housed art gallery and the Brazilian
cultural center are completely oriented to the Rhine.

02

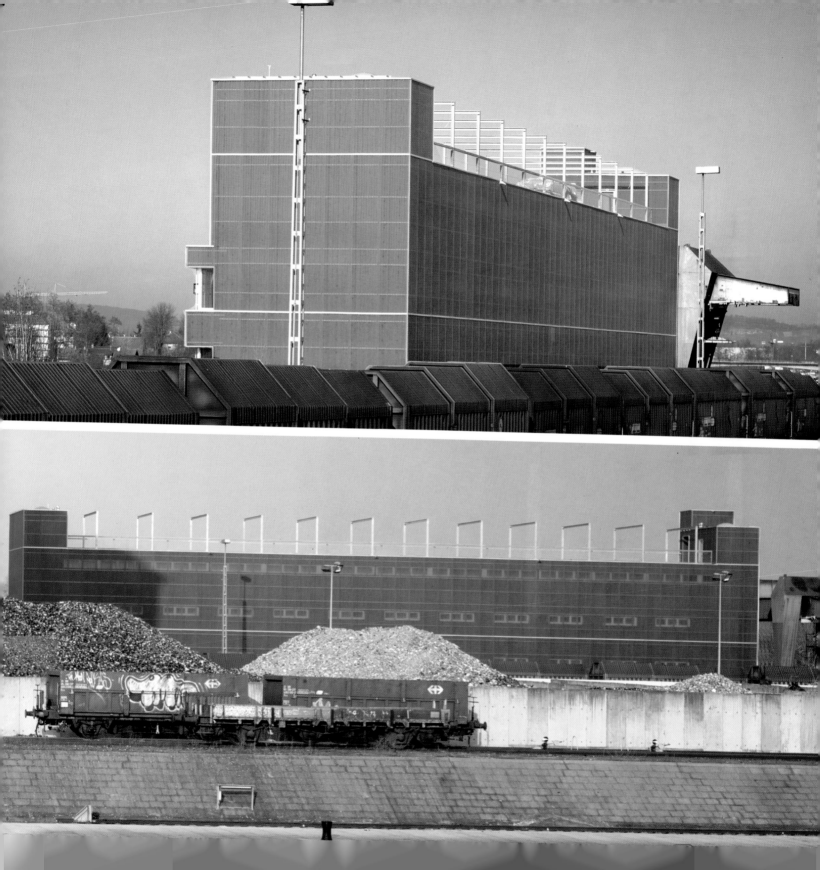

05

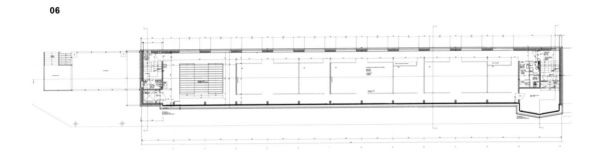

06

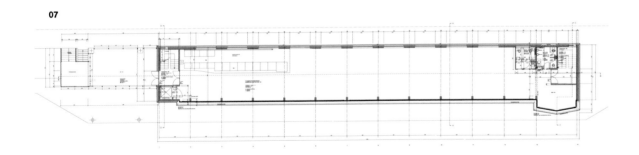

07

08

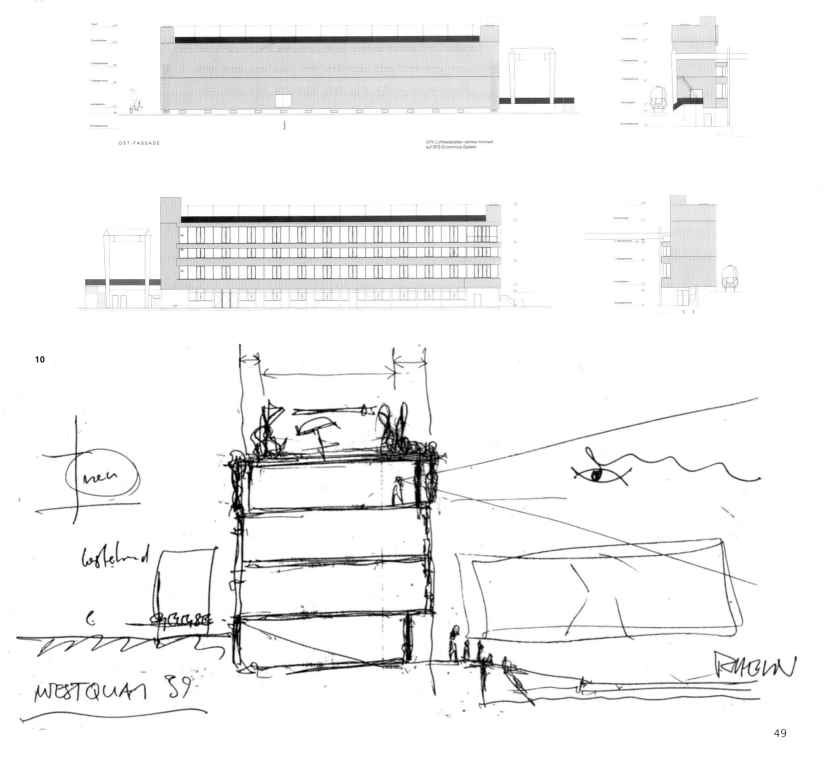

09

OST-FASSADE

GFK Lichtwellplatten vertikal montiert
auf SFS Economica System

Two-family house, 2005
Address: Am Lerchenbuck 17, 79379 Müllheim,
Germany. **Structural engineers:** Greschik + Falk +
Partner. **Client:** private. **Gross floor area:** 340 m².
Materials: polycarbonate (PC).

Unit of energy

ARCHITECTS: pfeifer roser kuhn architekten

This is not a classic two-family house, but a complex dovetailing of shared and individual, next to each other, above each other and across from each other. The residential structure for two family units rotates throughout the stories around a common hall, letting each unit enjoy all east-west orientations equally. The areas are independently connected using two open steps running in the opposite directions. The large hall gets lots of light through the roof, and the neighboring rooms benefit from it as well thanks to the interior windows surrounding the hall. The hall also functions as a large energy garden, supplying the whole house passively with sunlight energy. The material chosen for the transparent building envelope is made of polycarbonate elements and is characterized by low mass-per-surface area, resilience, simple construction, good sound absorption and a light emanating effect. The eave walls and roof surfaces of massive wood stacking elements are also enveloped. The massive single-leaf gable wall of light concrete bricks simultaneously provides mass for heat storage and ensures good sound insulation.

04

05

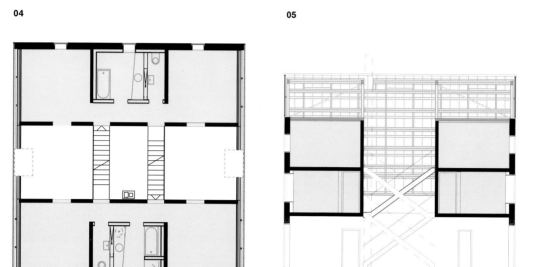

06

07

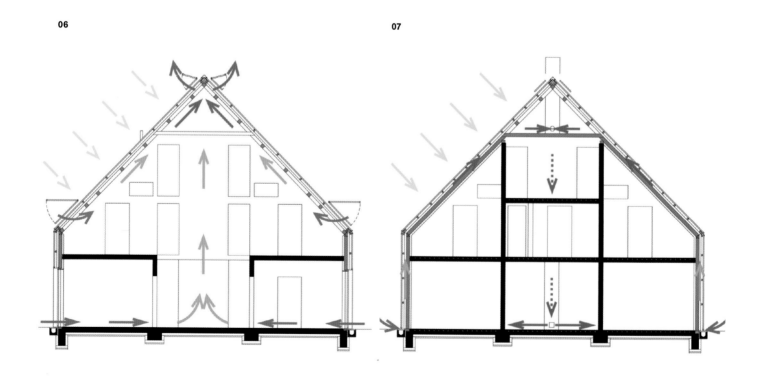

Center for continuing education and culture SÜD, 2008
Address: Pillenreuther Straße 147/149, Nuremberg, Germany. **Structural engineers:** IB Wetzel & von Seht. **Landscape architects:** Adler & Olesch. **Sponsored by:** Deutsche Bundesstiftung Umwelt. **Client:** City of Nuremberg. **Gross floor area:** 6,800 m². **Materials:** reinforced concrete frame, jamb-and-bar wooden façade with 3-layer glazing, bituterrazzo, industrial parquet, corrugate plates made of glass-reinforced plastic (GRP).

Plastic suite

ARCHITECTS: kuntz+manz architekten

"Südpunkt" (South Point) is a place for learning, culture and education in the south quarter of the city, housing a public library, a self-study center with a study group meeting room, a multifunctional event hall, a cafe and seminar rooms for adult education. The center represents an impulse for a structural change in the southern section of the city. This impulse is represented visually outside using the "glowing sign," which shows the visiting rate of the "passive learning institution"; between the opening hours of 9 am to 10 pm, 800 people visit SÜD on average. The façade of the top stories is characterized by an alternation of large openings. The highly insulated, opaque surfaces have GRP corrugated plate casing. The underlying color of the surface behind the casing varies with the viewing angle and sunlight conditions. Parts of the façade are backlit. The wavy surface of the GRP plates amplifies the optical effect.

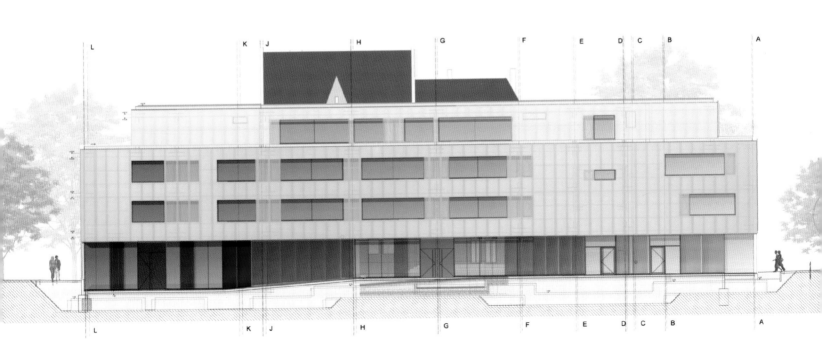

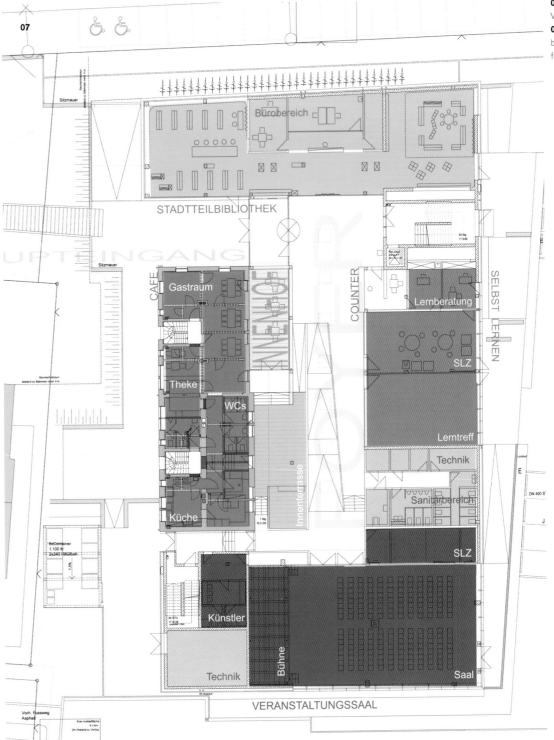

07

STADTTEILBIBLIOTHEK

Bürobereich

CAFE

Gastraum

Theke

WCs

Küche

Innenterrasse

COUNTER

Lernberatung

SLZ

Lerntreff

Technik

Sanitärbereich

SLZ

Künstler

Bühne

Technik

Saal

VERANSTALTUNGSSAAL

SELBST LERNEN

57

Production and assembly hall Behr Co., 2004
Address: Immenstädter Straße 36, 87544 Blaichach, Germany. **Client:** Firma Behr Technische Anlagen GmbH.
Gross floor area: 1,041 m². **Materials:** reinforced steel foundation, steel load-carrying frame, multiple web panels made of polycarbonate (PC).

Lift off

ARCHITECTS: Becker Architekten with Reiner Kliebhan

The production hall consists of a steel frame encased in multiple polycarbonate webbed panels, creating a light, diffused atmosphere. The translucent exterior skin reacts to various weather and light conditions, giving the building an opaque, mysterious external appearance. Especially in the evening or at night, the back-lit building acts as an advertising and image projection medium. A slight elevation above the floor gives the building a feeling of floating, additionally providing security in this flood-endangered area. The dynamic direction of light using RGB principles generates soft, timed color transitions whose palette is based on the four seasons. The composition accomplishes a reacquisition of a contaminated location in the middle of an undisturbed landscape. The production hall should enter into an exciting dialog with the planned office wing which will have a façade of aging silver-colored wood.

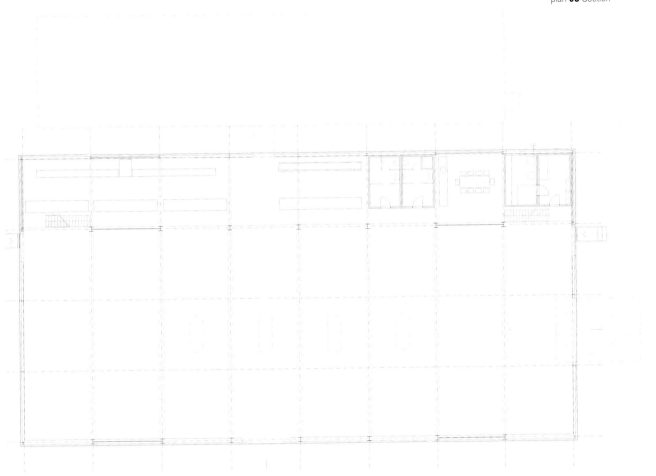

08

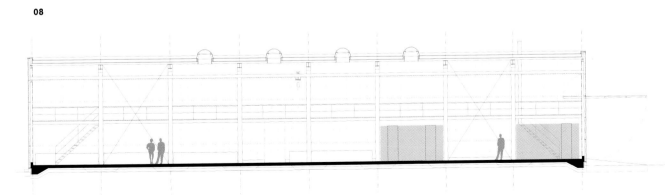

Center for group dynamics and institutional analyses (CDGAI), 2004
Address: Parc Scientifique du Sart Tilman, 9 rue du Bois Saint-Jean, 4102 Seraing, Belgium. **Structural engineers:** Ney & Partners. **Artist:** Jean Glibert. **Client:** CDGAI. **Gross floor area:** 333 m². **Materials:** rubber, perforated galvanized iron sheets, oriented strand board (OSB), Reglit, concrete, polycarbonate (PC).

Light-emitting drop

ARCHITECTS: Dethier & Associés

The new institute building contains offices, a library and meeting and conference rooms, all of which had to be realized on a small area and using low-cost building methods due to limited budget. Industrial fabrication methods were employed, including digitally-planned workflow for minimal time loss during construction and installation processes. The walls facing each other create a contrast: on the northern side, a massive wall, and on the southern side, a light steel frame covered by a polycarbonate sheet. This wall acts as a screen for the daytime shadow puppet play of tree silhouettes while filling all neighboring rooms with sunlight. At night, the whole building acts as a giant lantern. The roof surface is covered with rubber. Colorful canvases by Jean Glibert decorate the walls of the large rooms.

05

23m15

11m

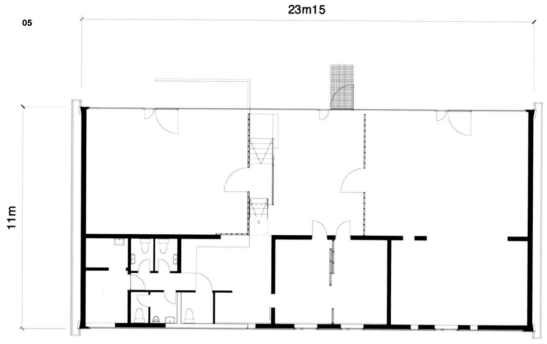

06

L.A. Design Center – Furniture showroom + exterior public events space, 2003
Address: 5595 S. Western Avenue, Los Angeles, CA 90047, USA. **Landscape architects:** Orange Street Studio. **Client:** Francisco and Alba Pinedo. **Owners:** Cisco Brothers. **Gross floor area:** 5,574 m² indoor, 1,858 m² outdoor. **Materials:** stainless steel (entry door, etc.), textured concrete, steel channel (interior and exterior bench), douglas fir (exterior screens), persforated steel grating (sliding gates), Polygal poly-carbonate (PC; canopies on exterior, divider on interior), polymethyl methacrylate (PMMA, "acrylic glass"; stair guardrail, partition walls).

Screen and green

ARCHITECTS: John Friedman and Alice Kimm Architects

This rehabilitation of two derelict masonry warehouses created 5,574 m² of interior furniture showrooms and 1,858 m² of exterior public space. The project has cata-lyzed revitalization in South Los Angeles. By introducing a varied palette of materials and colors that are lightly juxtaposed atop the existing buildings, the architects created a distinctive and iconic facility, which is simul-taneously inclusive and welcoming. The interior is illu-minated by skylights and light hues are introduced by sandblasted masonry and wood. A steel and acrylic stair inserted into a new opening to the second floor forms the focal point of a new foyer. The most extensive trans-formations occur on the exterior, where polycarbonate panels create a billboard for the entire facility, and ce-ment board in varying shades of green speaks to the city's effort to "green" its streets.

01

02

04

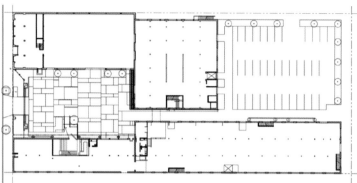

01 Foyer and reception **02** Billboard and fence **03** Public event space **04** First floor plan **05** Phasing of material applications to event site **06** Showroom

05

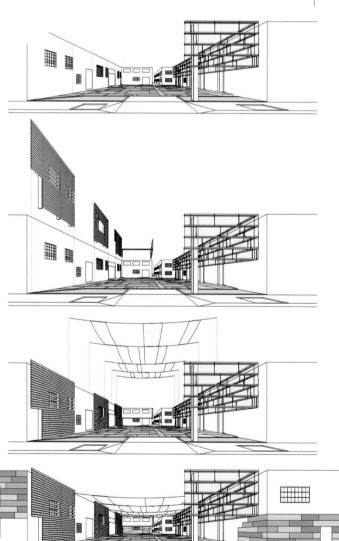

Sports and culture center Crystal, 2006
Address: Holmbladsgade 71, 2300 Copenhagen S, Denmark. **Client:** Copenhagen Municipality, LOA – Danish Foundation for Culture and Sports Facilities. **Gross floor area:** 3,400 m². **Materials:** steel, wood, panels made of polycarbonate (PC; façade).

Urban green

ARCHITECTS: b&k+ Arno Brandlhuber,
Dorte Mandrup Arkitekter

The new building will be used for a variety of daily sport and cultural activities such as concerts and theater performances. The dynamic landscape that unfolds inside lets these activities take place on different levels, while remaining in visual contact with each other. The most pronounced feature is a large translucent membrane that stretches between the sports arena and the culture center. The irregular, trailing form of the space results from the continuum created with the four walls of the neighboring buildings, the regulations guiding the structure and the program requirements. Steel and timber covered with opalescent polycarbonate panels with a low U-value were used as building materials. The translucent cover creates excellent daylight conditions and, together with the green flooring, hints at an open-air experience. The translucent outer skin dissolves the volume of the building, and at night, makes the structure appear as a glowing crystal.

04

01 View over the roof **02** Façade **03** Interior zoom towards court-yards **04** Situation **05** Section **06** Ground floor plan **07** Section **08** Exterior view

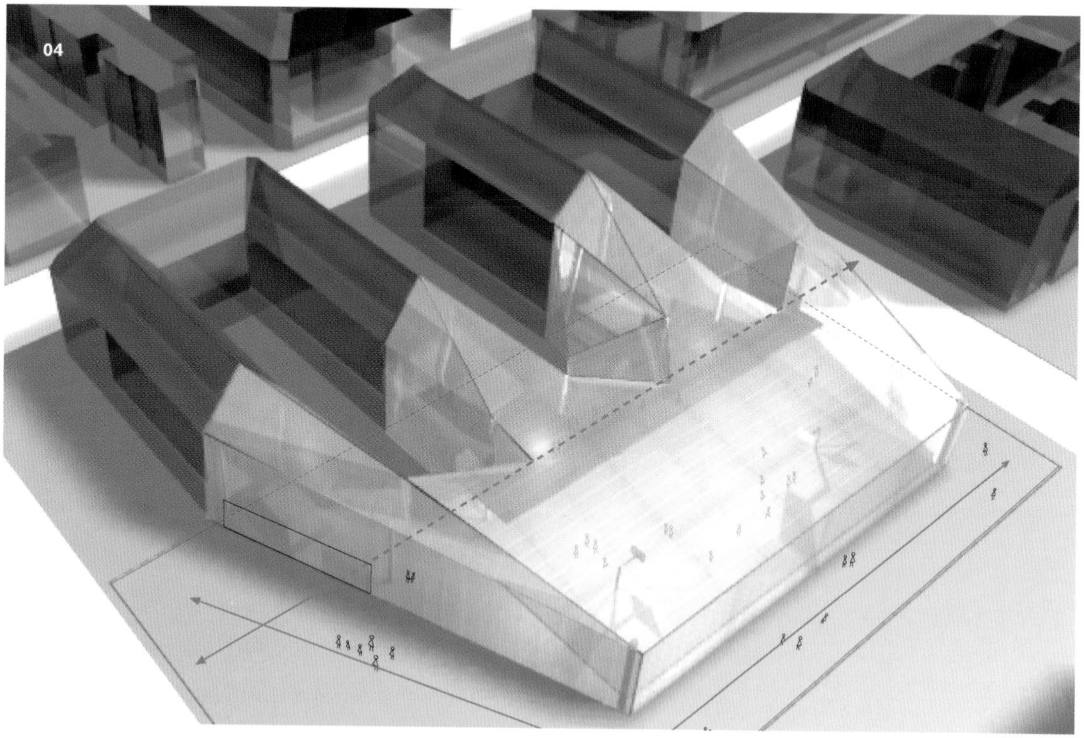

05

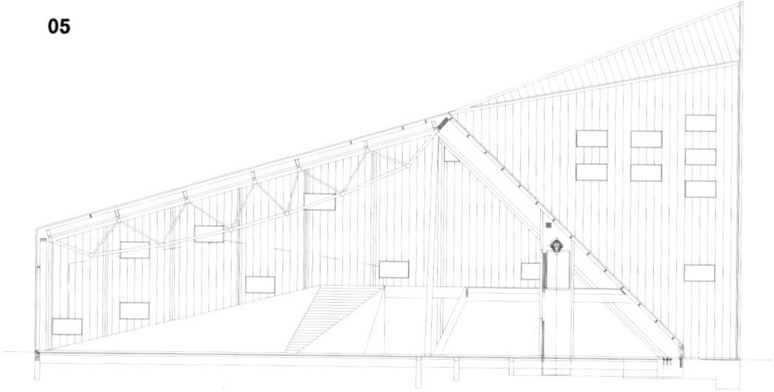

06

ground floor

1	sports floor
2	café
3	office
4	bar & info desk
5	kitchen
6	change room
7	storage
8	theatre
9	dance room

0 m ——— 10 m

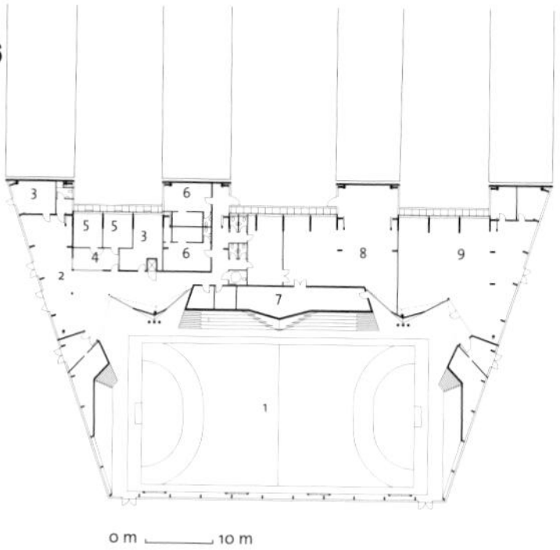

07

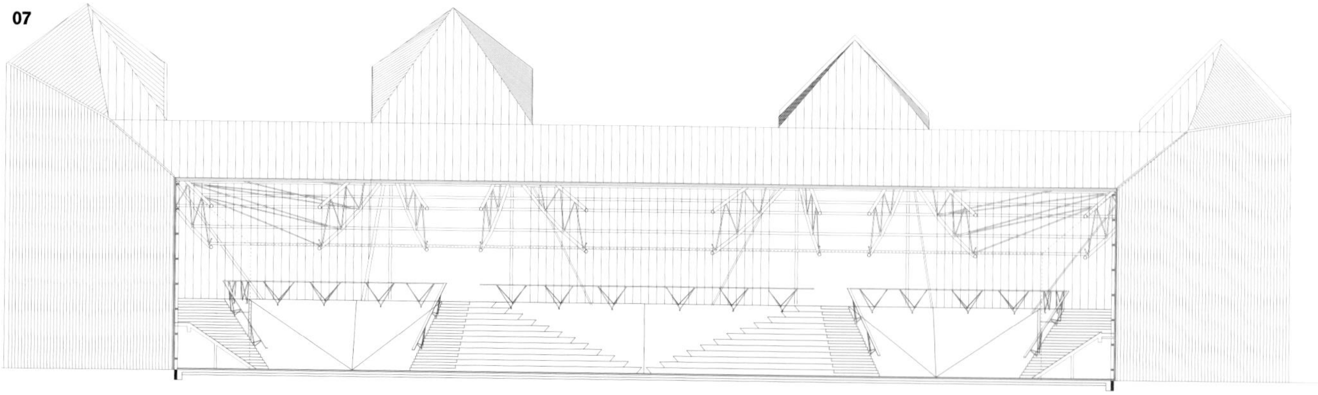

01

Single-family house in Zdarky, 2003
Address: Zdarky – Hronov, Czech Republic. **Client:** private. **Gross floor area:** 107.6 m². **Materials:** monolithic concrete, wooden plates, plates made of polyvinyl chloride (PVC, "vinyl").

Neoplastic architecture
ARCHITECTS: ARCHTEAM

The house is located in the middle of a scenic countryside, and its design is in the spirit of a traditional country house. The simple building layout is complemented with a garage and an outhouse built using wood and plastic plates. The house appears severe from its street façade, but opens up towards the garden through a large glazed face. This project employed low-cost architectural means. Opaque plastic plates that were used for handrails and moving shutters play a significant role. While used as a secondary motif on the main building, the PVC panels become the main design element on the secondary structures. The garage and outhouse walls are built from opaque plastic plates. These provide an adequate optical cover while partially covering and revealing the two buildings. The free-standing garage has some feeling of continuity. Upon entering it, an opaque red plastic wall appears in front of the driver. The opening of the space occurs only after the initial optical beholding of the material.

02

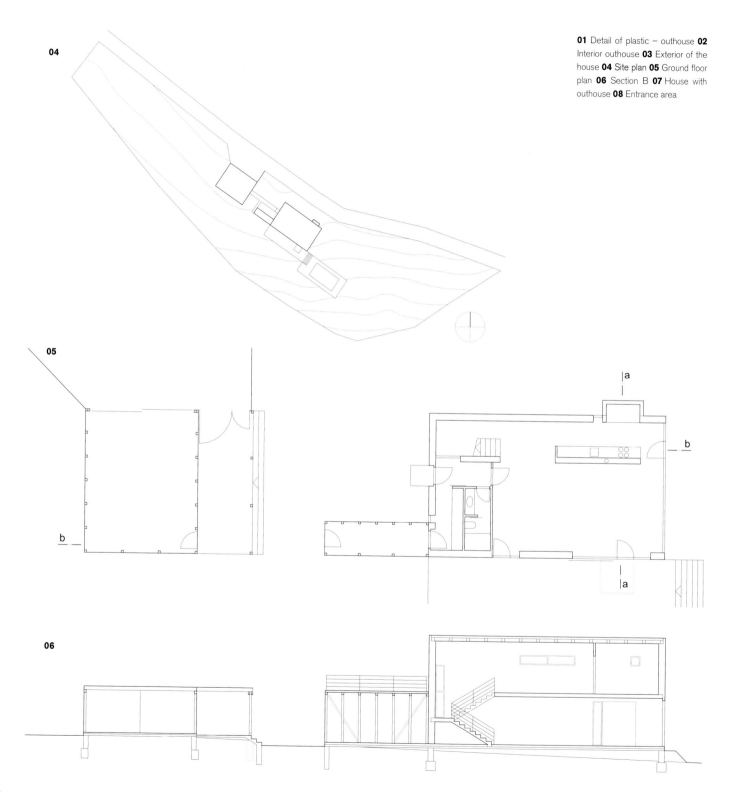

04

01 Detail of plastic – outhouse **02** Interior outhouse **03** Exterior of the house **04** Site plan **05** Ground floor plan **06** Section B **07** House with outhouse **08** Entrance area

05

a

b

b

a

06

76

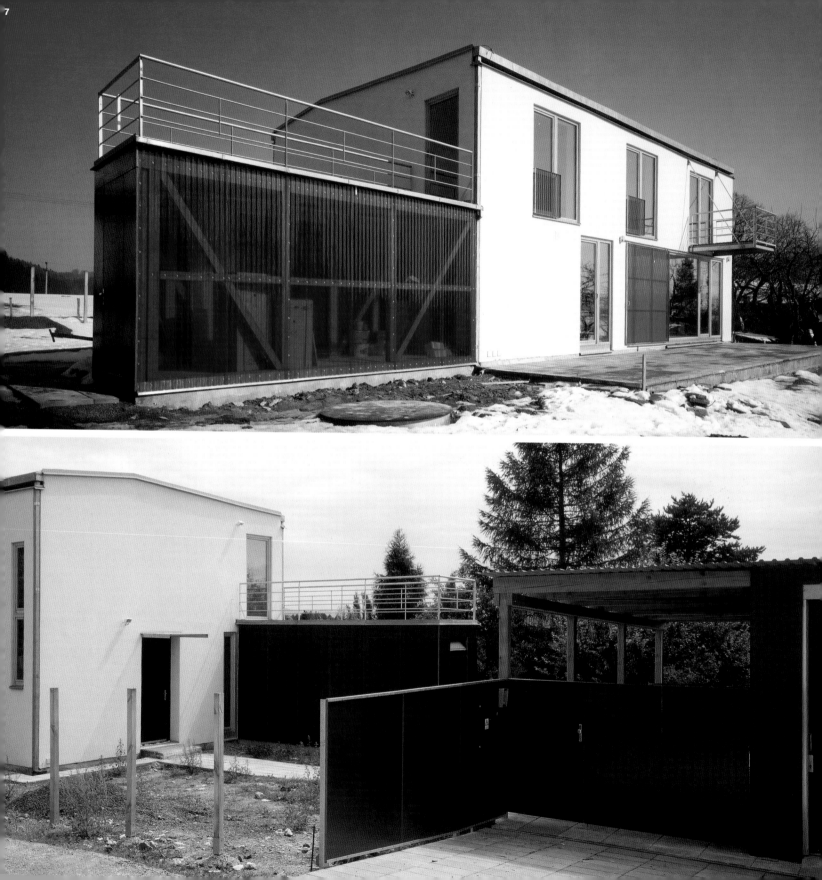

01

**New Camp Nou Stadium for FC Barcelona, 2012
Address:** Avinguda Aristides Maillol, s/n 08028,
Barcelona, Spain. **Collaborating sports architect
(competition):** AFL. **Client:** FC Barcelona. **Gross floor
area:** 180,000 m². **Materials:** steel, concrete, glass,
polycarbonate (PC).

Gaudiamus

ARCHITECTS: Foster + Partners

The stadium, already the largest in Europe, will be en-
larged even more to accommodate over 106,000 fans
and remodeled with extensive new facilities including
hospitality and public areas. A new mosaic enclosure
composed of translucent panels in the colors of the
FC Barcelona club will act as rain screen around the
stadium sides, allowing naturally ventilated concourse
areas. The mosaic pattern continues over the roof, were
a cable net structure spans across the stadium and is
stretched inside a compression ring above the outer
edge of the seating bowl. The enclosure is to include
photovoltaic panels to harvest solar energy. At night,
lighting will make it glow in bright colors. The remodeled
stadium retains the essential elements of the original
Camp Nou, like the characteristic asymmetric seating
bowl, designed by architects Francesc Mitjans-Miró,
García Barbon and Soteras Mauri, which was inaugu-
rated in 1957.

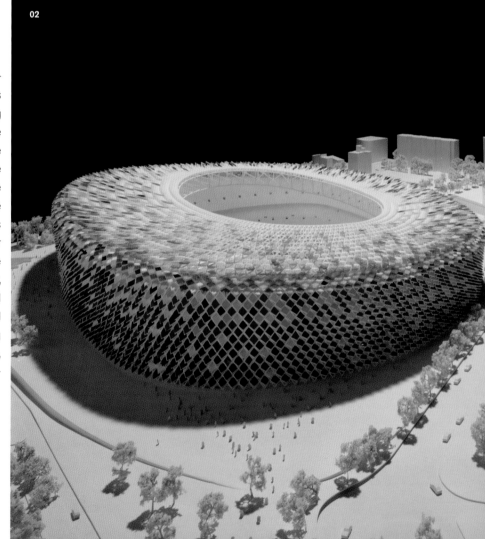

02

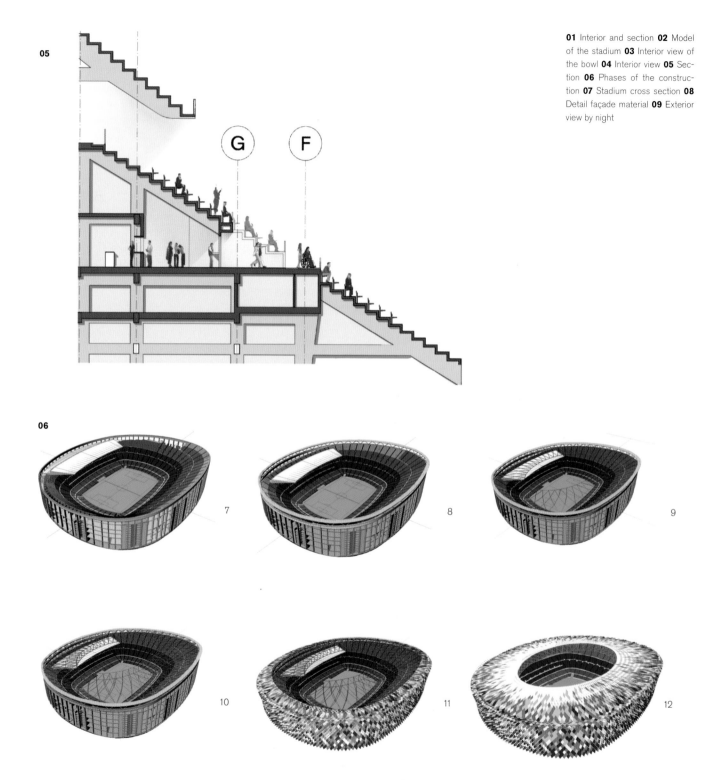

05

G F

06

7

8

9

10

11

12

09

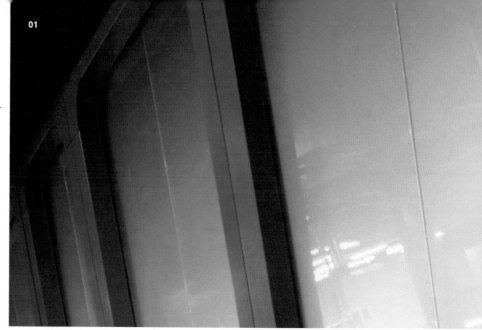

Visitor walkway Voestalpine, 2006
Address: Voestalpinestraße 1, 4020 Linz, Austria.
Client: Voest Alpine. **Gross floor area:** variable. **Materials:** steel, glass, plates made of polymethyl methacrylate (PMMA, "acrylic glass"), mats made of polyvinyl chloride (PVC, "vinyl"), foam plastic.

Visitor platform

ARCHITECTS: Caramel Architekten with f. stiper

The conglomerate involved in raw materials processing was once viewed as unprofitable, rigid and unfriendly to the environment, but has meanwhile succeeded in becoming one of Austria's exemplary businesses whose high quality steel products are manufactured under strict environmental protection guidelines. To present its activities to the interested public ranging from school classes to business partners, architecture office Caramel was charged with developing visitor platforms. Basic modules allow creation of various layouts and viewing formats. They are assembled onsite (placed or hung) using easily transportable prefabricated uniform pieces. Back-lit sitting and standing platforms form a multirowed assembly of viewing spaces with unhindered perspective even from the seats in the back. Following a presentation on the screen, the glass panes can be turned from opaque to clear, allowing direct observation of the production line.

04

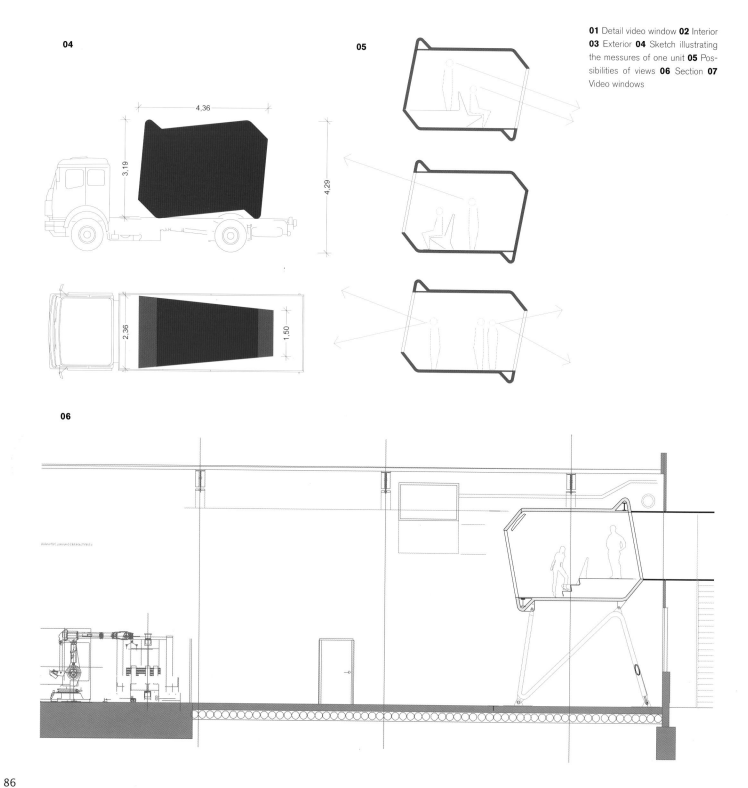

4,36

3,19

2,36

1,50

05

01 Detail video window **02** Interior
03 Exterior **04** Sketch illustrating
the messures of one unit **05** Pos-
sibilities of views **06** Section **07**
Video windows

06

Restaurant, cocktail bar and club the Mansion, 2004
Address: Hobbemastraat 2, 1071ZA Amsterdam, The Netherlands. **Team:** Rob Wagemans, Joris Angevaare, Erik van Dillen. **Client:** Andy Martin. **Gross floor area:** 1,300 m². **Materials:** Chrome steel, wood, brushed, stainless steel, nappa leather, ostrich synthetic leather, Corian acrylic-bound solid surface, polyvinyl chloride (PVC, "vinyl").

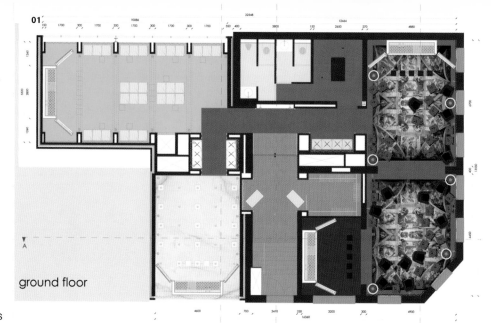

ground floor

Michelangelo's dining

ARCHITECTS: Concrete Architectural Associates

Concrete was asked to create a contemporary, luxurious, classic, sexy, chic and warm gentlemen's club in a stately location of a former restaurant. They decided to combine the already grand look of the building with many different environments linked by several elements that are present throughout the space, like the synthetic cornices made by Proga Kunststoffen. Most walls are covered with Viscaya lily pattern on vinyl wallpaper, a classic pattern combined with a modern material. The wallpaper color varies in accordance to the color scheme of the room it is used in. Most of the tabletops are made of Corian with synthetic, mirrored cornices as edge detail: off-white in the cocktail bar, tea rose in the Rosé Room and vanilla in the entrée. In the Black Bar most of the ceiling displays a modern interpretation of the Sistine chapel ceiling mural. A special synthetic material that is usually used for light cases for large outdoor advertisements was employed for the backlit ceiling. To mask the harshness of the outside world, the windows in this room are foiled with a dark grey vinyl and draped by black lace curtains.

01 Ground floor plan **02 + 03** Bar **04** Dining room

dv atelier, 2004
Address: Gottesackerstraße 21, 85221 Dachau, Germany. **Client:** Dorothea Voitländer, Konrad Deffner.
Gross floor area: 446 m². **Materials:** concrete, glass, wood, fiber-reinforced polymer (FRP, fiber-reinforced plastic).

Invisible cap

ARCHITECTS: deffner voitländer architekten

An old linden tree is the focus of a residential and office building that stands in Dachau's center. It is not only that the general building plan and all its rooms are oriented in relation to the tree, but the façade additionally carries an image of its branches as they appear in winter. The façade consists of hand-laminated panels of translucent, glass fiber-reinforced plastic. The tree motif is continuous, non-repetitive, printed on special paper and applied like a tattoo into the fiber reinforced plastics skin. A complex interaction between the tree, its shadow and the artificial silhouette comes about through this structure. The original, shadow and image come together in the course of the day and the year cycles as a constantly-changing collage, camouflaging the house and the area surrounding the tree.

04

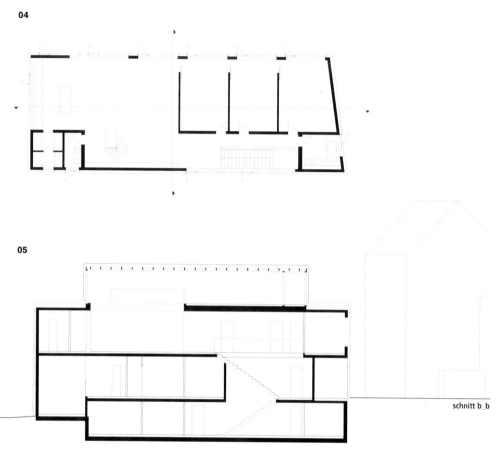

05

schnitt b_b

06

07

**Residential, office and kindergarten
MULTIFUNK®, 2006
Address:** Pieter Holmplein, IJburg, Amsterdam, The
Netherlands. **Client:** Ymere Ontwikkeling BV, Lingotto
vastgoed BV. **Gross floor area:** 20,250 m². **Materials:**
concrete, aluminum, brick, recycled polyethylene (PE)
and polypropylene (PP, polypropene) from crates,
bottle tops, etc.

Waste utilization plant

ARCHITECTS: ANA architecten

Multifunk® is a flexible building that can easily change
its functions. It can be gradually transformed from a
residential building into an office building and vice
versa. Since the complex consists of a fixed structure
that can be freely filled in, the flexibility of the concept
does not only leave room to mix or alternate functions,
but it can also meet the different needs for space that
these functions require. The building stands on Steiger-
eiland which forms the main entrance to a new city
quarter with mixed-use area for housing and offices.
The building mediates between these contrasting areas
and brings together the large and small scale elements
on the island. The recycled material corresponds to the
second life that the Multifunk® building can and will
have by definition. The unique material KLP® by Lank-
horst Recycling BV gives the complex both an exclusive
and an informal feel. The plastic has many advantages.
It is environmentally friendly, durable, maintenance-free,
splinter-free and easy to apply and doesn't contain any
harmful substances.

02

01 Overall view **02** Detail plastic cladding **03** Northeast elevation **04** Fragment southwest elevation **05** Court façade **06** Street façade **07 + 08** Concept for the façade

07

zwart gevelvlak volgt grens tussen openbaar en prive

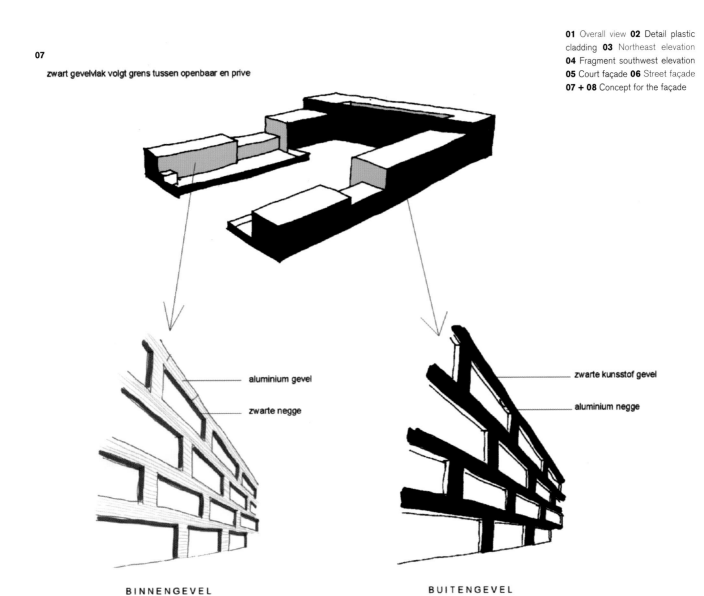

aluminium gevel

zwarte negge

zwarte kunsstof gevel

aluminium negge

BINNENGEVEL

BUITENGEVEL

08

Children's Nursery on the Green, 2004
Address: Thorncliffe Road, Middlesex UB2 5RN, United Kingdom. **Evironmental engineers:** Max Fordham. **Structural engineers:** HRW. **Client:** NDNA London Regional Centers. **Gross floor area:** 726 m². **Materials:** timber inner structure with eternit multiclad; outer roof with steel frame and glass-reinforced plastic (GRP).

Sheltered childhood

ARCHITECTS: Cottrell & Vermeulen

Children occupy spaces differently from adults – a difference that predominates in Cottrell & Vermeulen's investigation of affordable, child-friendly architecture. Children need outdoor space for play; they become restless indoors and escape through unlocked windows; they lie on their backs and look at the ceiling or hide under furniture. The oversized roof in this nursery provides bright external "rooms" that open up onto the interior spaces, effectively doubling the accommodation on rainy days. The landscape is conceived as a series of safe rooms, each providing varied activities. By creating a large, sheltered children's territory, the center is easier to manage and more fun to use. To achieve the translucency of the rainscreen "tent", Building Regulations required the product to be strong enough to walk on for maintenance and have class "O" fire-resistance. For this purpose the architects used Hartington Conway Profile GRP class "O".

05

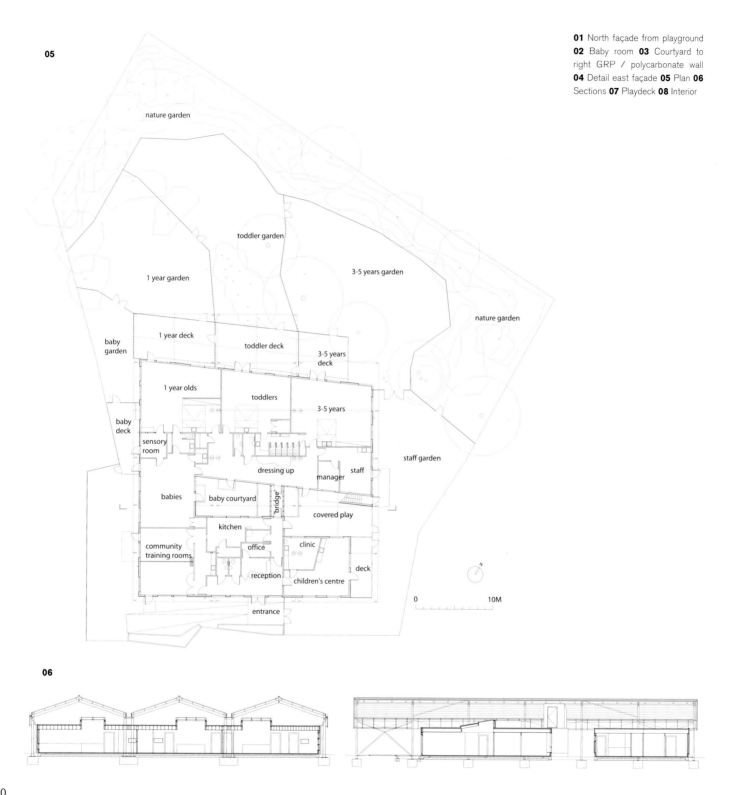

nature garden

toddler garden

1 year garden

3-5 years garden

nature garden

baby garden

1 year deck

toddler deck

3-5 years deck

baby deck

1 year olds

toddlers

3-5 years

sensory room

dressing up

staff garden

manager

staff

babies

baby courtyard

"bridge"

covered play

kitchen

community training rooms

office

clinic

reception

children's centre

deck

entrance

0   10M

06

Plastic house, 2002
Address: Tokyo, Japan. **Structural engineers:** Kajima Design. **Client:** private. **Gross floor area:** 172.75 m². **Materials:** steel, fiber-reinforced polymer (FRP, fiber-reinforced plastic).

Unconcrete

ARCHITECTS: Kengo Kuma & Associates

The house for a mother (writer) and a son (photographer) stands in the center of the city and various parts of "living" are open to the urban condition. The question of how to escape from the massiveness of a concrete box has been Kengo Kuma's pursuit for many years. Concrete has fit the 20th century so well, that other local methods of construction have been abandoned. Therefore, the search for a substitute material is not a mere formal proposal, but an attempt to suggest a 'principle of living' that replaces the fundamental demands for "strength" and "security" of the 20th century. In Edo period, wood was the material that lead to tenant housing creating the cityscape. FRP was employed for the project to create a new relationship between inhabitants and the city. FRP is a 4 mm-thick material molded into various shapes. Combining these shapes creates relationships of different qualities were created – sometimes it appears like rice paper and sometimes like bamboo, depending on the quality of fibers contained. Instead of using bead at joints, butyl rubber and plastic screws were selected for the construction to not detract from this quality.

04

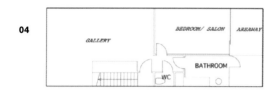

GALLERY

BEDROOM/ SALON

AREAWAY

BATHROOM

WC

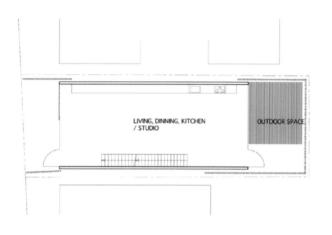

LIVING, DINNING, KITCHEN / STUDIO

OUTDOOR SPACE

05

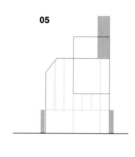

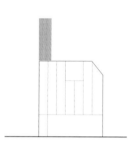

West Elevation

East Elevation

BEDROOM

BATHROOM

BEDROOM

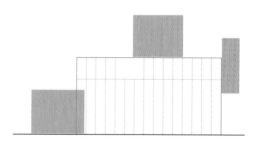

North Elevation

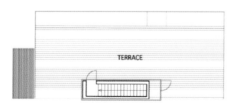

TERRACE

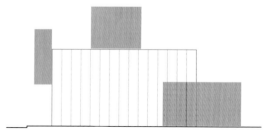

Temporary exhibition pavilions Mobile Museums, 2007
Address: changing (Berlin, Barcelona, Vienna). **Client:** Public Art Lab, Susa Pop, Hans Jörg Wiegner. **Gross floor area:** 10 m². **Materials:** Kömacell polyvinyl chloride (PVC, "vinyl") integrated foam panels.

Encapsulated

ARCHITECTS: Gruber + Popp Architekten BDA with Hans Jörg Wiegner

The idea behind Mobile Museums is to experience familiar locations anew through a temporary occupation which changes their structure and atmosphere. Using the modular construction kit of recycled PVC, artists can construct their own museum with a maximal size of 10 m². The modular concept enables creation of accessible room structures. The outer envelope corresponds to the inner atmospheric space. Mobile Museums offer various ways of rethinking the concepts of exhibition space and museum. The museum as a modular system allows flexible architecture design and achieving a unity of artwork and space. PVC integrated foam panels are characterized by their low weight and simultaneously high level of stability in relation to elasticity, pull and push loads. No additional costs are involved in construction of cubes: the integrated foam panels carry all static loads.

01 Top shot of the Mobile Museums on the Potsdamer Platz, Berlin
02 Mobile Museums on the Potsdamer Platz, Berlin 03 Interior
pavilion Franka Hörnschemeyer
04 Floor plan 05 Interior pavilion
Hans Jörg Wiegner

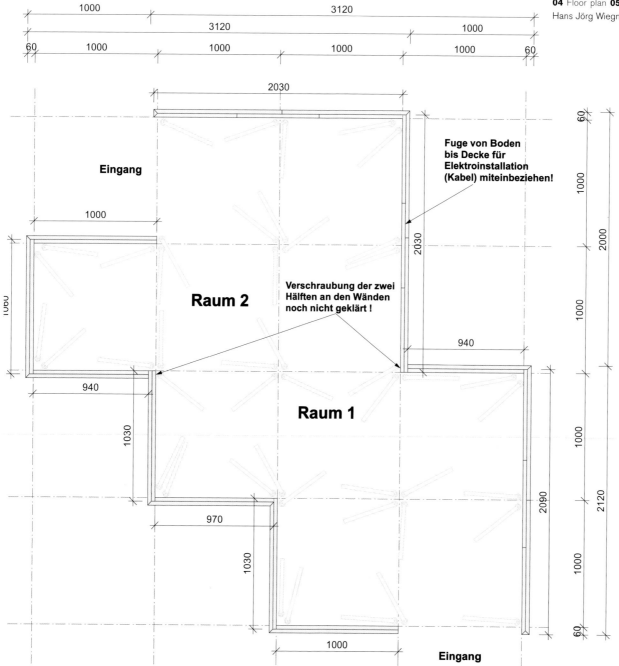

Eingang

Raum 2

Raum 1

Eingang

Fuge von Boden
bis Decke für
Elektroinstallation
(Kabel) miteinbeziehen!

Verschraubung der zwei
Hälften an den Wänden
noch nicht geklärt !

01

Urban Structure Museum (K-Museum), 1996
Address: Tokyo, Japan. **Client:** Tokyo Metropolitan
Government. **Gross floor area:** 245.4 m². **Materials:**
aluminum, mirror-surface and gold-colored stainless panels, concrete, fiber-reinforced polymer (FRP,
fiber-reinforced plastic), honey comb panels made of
polymethyl methacrylate (PMMA, "acrylic glass").

Repossession

ARCHITECTS: Makoto Sei Watanabe

The construction of the new city center started in the
1980s amid the so-called business boom bubble. Its in-
frastructure had been nearly completed and superstruc-
tures were about to go up when the recession of the
early 1990s put an end to everything. The center of the
new city remained a vast empty space, a meaningless
void that is neither urban nor rural. The K-Museum located in this context devoid of any identity brings quality
of architecture into this quantity of failure. The building is
meant to be a model of the city itself, a moment of con-
stant change symbolized by its overall unstable appearance. On the interior, walls and ceilings are constructed
using a newly developed material called "acry honeycomb", which consists of two acrylic sheets sandwiching
an aluminum honeycomb. The silver honeycomb inside
is illuminated using back lighting. The structure sitting
on top of the building is made of semi-transparent FRP
and functions as a skylight in the daytime, and a source
of illumination at night. At the dawn of the 21st century,
this area awoke from a long sleep and is becoming one
of Tokyo's centers of commerce.

01 Organ on the roof **02** Toilets **03** Exterior detail **04** Exterior **05** Interior
06 Detail, exterior material **07** Detail, interior material

02

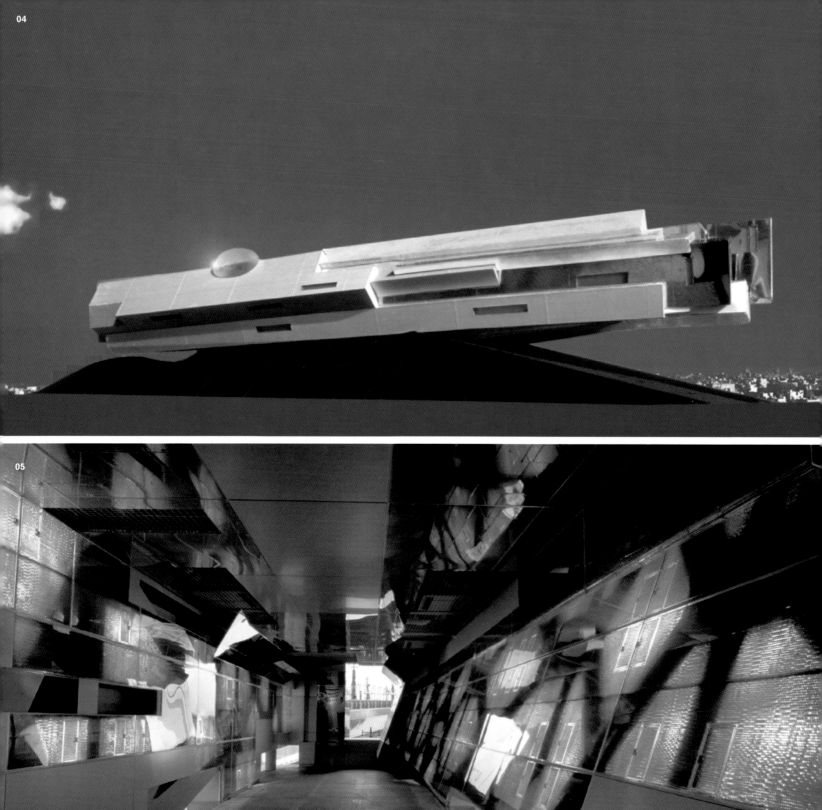

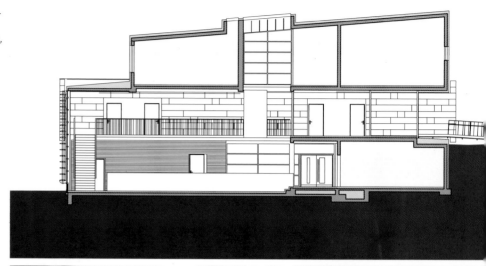

Extension for the Schwarzenbergstraße Special Education School, 2005
Address: Schwarzenbergstraße 72, Hamburg-Harburg, Germany. **Landscape architects:** arbos Landschaftsarchitekten. **Client:** Municipality of Hamburg. **Gross floor area:** 1,950 m². **Materials:** blind clinker, plaster, oak, fair-faced concrete, metal, surface plates made of Resopal high pressure laminates (HPL, coated wood panels, "laminate").

Brute force resistance

ARCHITECTS: Niemann Architekten

The free-standing new building completes the heterogeneous school ensemble, erected in the course of a century. The hillside location allowed one side of the building to be buried. The building has compact, almost square proportions. The individual volumes housing classrooms, secondary spaces and the auditorium are arranged around a two-story void containing the break hall. The plinth is covered in clinker masonry, while the upper story is encased in colorful plastic plates. The cellar is plastered white. The use of plastic panels in the construction of the school building was motivated by its robustness. By using laminate on various mounting plates, it was possible to use the same surface for different requirements. The HLP used on the façade is weather-resistant. Inside, the plate is made fire resistant using embedded glass granules, and additionally provides acoustic damping. Last, but not least, plastics offer a range of saturated colors to choose from.

01 Section **02** Façade **03** Break hall

Junky Hotel, 2004
Address: Maliebaan, Utrecht, The Netherlands.
Structural engineers: Bartels ingenieursburo Utrecht.
Client: Public health department of Utrecht. **Gross floor area:** 1,000 m². **Materials:** Resopal high pressure laminates (HPL, coated wood panels, "laminate").

Climbing aid

ARCHITECTS: Bararchitects

In the main monumental building of the Junky Hotel, there are spaces for 22 occupants. It is a public structure made out of two identically mirrored buildings behind a single façade. The central corridor, clad with high-pressure laminate with ivy prints, connects the various supervisory rooms and houses the necessary storage. The entrees on both sides of the supervisory spaces are connected to the two residential groups. The living room, recreation room, and the sleeping quarters are organized along the front and back façades. The extra space is taken by a service module that attends every floor. On each floor there are different service programs and different left-over spaces. Because the heights of the volumes are not aligned with the floor heights of the main building, the autonomy of the composition is strengthened. The different modules give every floor its own spatial identity. The ivy-print cladding eases the homeless addicts' difficult transition from the outside to the inside.

04

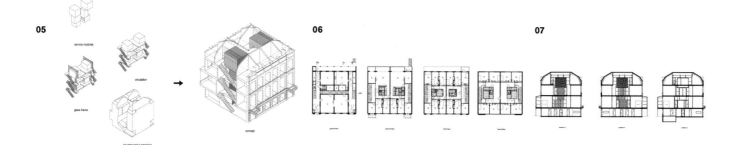

05

service modules

circulation

glass frame

housing and supervision

concept

06

07

Department store, spa and corporate headquarters, Armani / Ginza Tower, 2007
Address: Ginza, Tokyo, Japan. **Client:** Giorgio Armani.
Gross floor area: 6,000 m². **Materials:** glass, steel, concrete, polymethyl methacrylate (PMMA, "acrylic glass").

Intimate evanescence

ARCHITECTS:
Massimiliano Fuksas and Doriana Mandrelli

The Armani / Ginza Tower had to reflect not only the atmosphere of the Italian designer's atelier, but also his aesthetic code and his personal image. Luxury with restrained elegance, absolute modernity and an enduring style had to be translated into the Armani architectural style. The designer's vision and relentless research into materials, together with his use of delicate, translucent and radiant colors are all key factors that prompted this design. Correspondingly, the architecture was developed using new textures and materialization and dematerilization of space with the help of light. In addition to bamboo, gossamer screens as light as silk, shafts of white light, translucence and intimacy act as the main motifs. Giorgio Armani himself was closely involved in the design process, always ready to engage with all concept modifications.

05

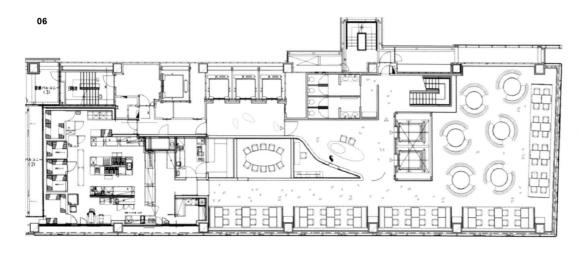

06

07

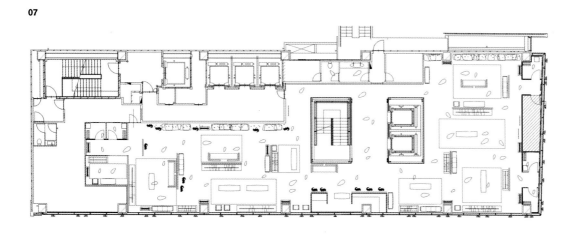

Museum Plagiarius, 2007
Address: Bahnhofstraße 11, 42651 Solingen, Germany.
Client: Sanierungsgesellschaft Südliche Innenstadt
Solingen. **Gross floor area:** 1,100 m². **Materials:** steel,
concrete, glass, tracks and profiles made of polyvinyl
chloride (PVC, "vinyl").

Pirates and Plato

ARCHITECTS: Angelis Reinhard Architekturbüro

The museum complements the product design forum,
and attempts to illustrate the difference between original products and plagiarisms taken from various trade
sectors using about 250 exhibits. The building is an addition to a former warehouse in the southern section of
Solingen. The foyer frame gives the original building a
respectable appearance and follows the outlines of the
existing traditional silhouette of the half-timbered house
with street-facing gables, at the same time turning it
into something completely new. The unusual choice of
materials, the linear but asymmetric, non-static façade
accented using irregular window placement as well as
a protective envelope that brings the roof and the side
walls together all distort the original form to the point
that the "half-timbered gable house" seems to be not
more than an inspiration for the final product. The museum's subject is conveyed by the building itself: independent search for form through mimicry.

04

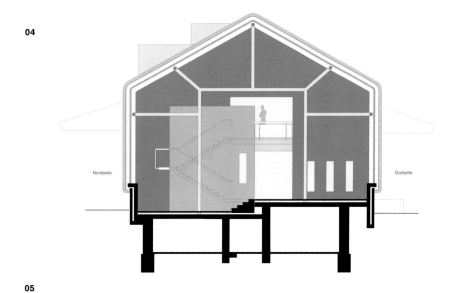

Nordseite

Südseite

05

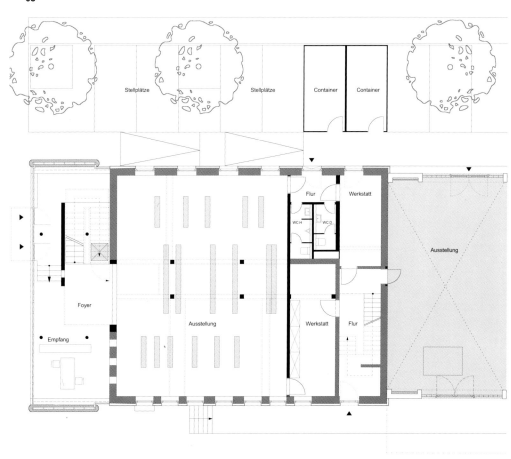

Stellplätze

Stellplätze

Container

Container

Flur

Werkstatt

WC H

WC D

Ausstellung

Foyer

Ausstellung

Werkstatt

Flur

Empfang

CURVATURE

Office NTT International, 2008
Address: Space Business Park, Noordwijk, The Netherlands. **Studies:** Technology Transfer Program of the European Space Agency. **Client:** NTT International bv. **Gross floor area:** 750 m². **Materials:** glass, foam made of Polyvinyl chloride (PVC, "vinyl"), carbon fiber reinforced plastic (CFRP).

Touch down / stand up

DESIGN: Fritz Gampe
ARCHITECTS: Dil en Bonazzi Architecten

The idea of transferring a self-sufficient building from space travel research to earth appeared after the ecological catastrophes of the 1990s. The advances in the high-strength carbon fiber-reinforced plastic production methods enable the creation of self-supporting forms, which in the case of NTT offices are two spherical elements with likewise spherical windows set against one another. The precise division of load is combined with consistent minimization of the weight of the building's volume and the self-supporting structure reduces the mass to about 15%. Another ecological aspect of the project is the novel manufacturing process of the carbon fibers, which reduces carbon dioxide emissions to 10% in comparison to conventional construction materials. The resin phenol used to the sandwich panels additionally makes the structure fireproof. NTT itself manufactures all the necessary construction materials. Thus, a building is created which in addition to its primary function of housing offices, also serves as an emblem for the owner's product, an experimental prototype for future standardized production, and an example of applied transfer of technology.

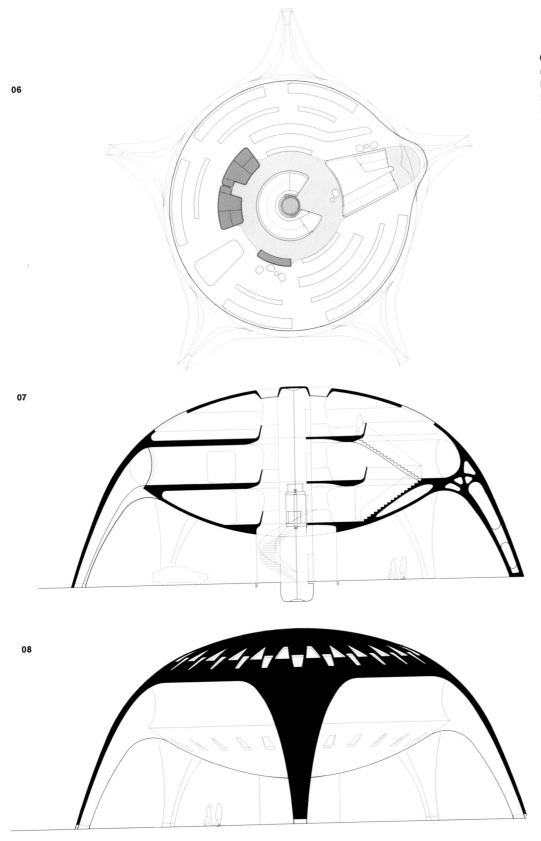

06

07

08

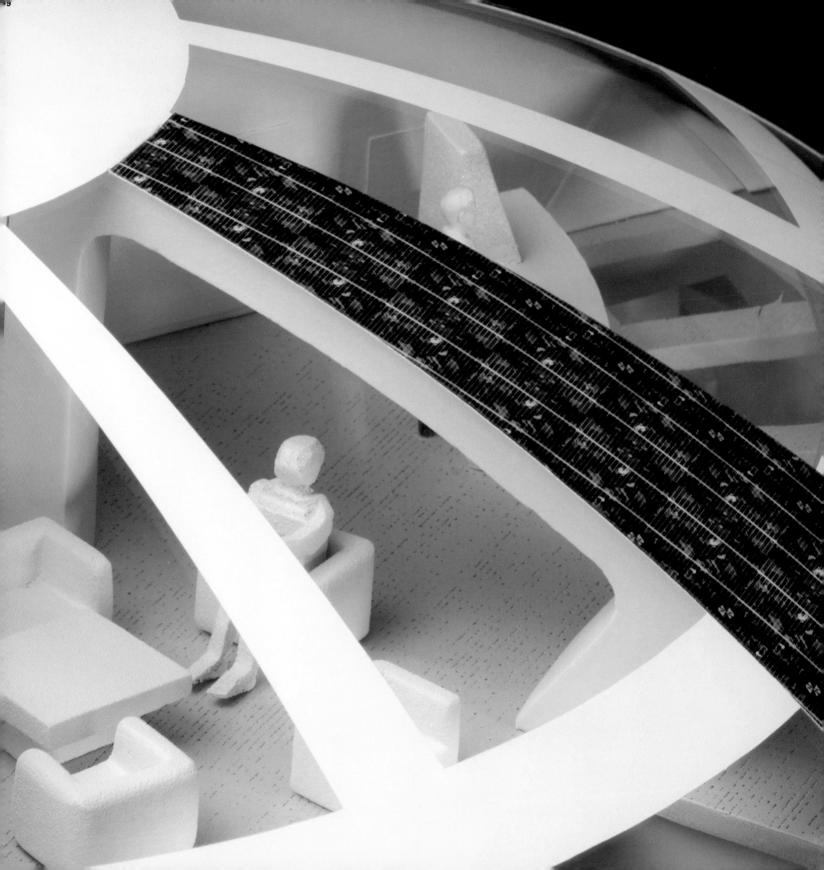

Museum Kunsthaus Graz, 2003
Address: Südtiroler Platz 2, 8020 Graz, Austria.
BIX media façade: realities:united. **Client:** Kunsthaus Graz. **Gross floor area:** 13,100 m². **Materials:** steel, concrete, glass, polymethyl methacrylate (PMMA, "acrylic glass").

Friendly alien

ARCHITECTS: Spacelab – Peter Cook, Colin Fournier

Positioned on the bank of the Mur, the "Friendly Alien," as the architects have named it, is a landmark. The biomorphic body clearly defines itself apart from its architectonic environment. At the same time, the building feeds into the urban space, initiating a far more complex dialog than is normally expected from a traditional "white cube" museum. The lustrous bubble appears to originate in the surrounding historical architectural milieu. In the daytime, the 1,200 smooth, dark, glistening acrylic glass plates contrast with the surrounding red brick roofs, while at night, 930 ring-shaped fluorescent lamps radiate from behind the plastic surface. These are the pixels of the BIX media façade, which are controlled by a central computer and can be individually smoothly dimmed. The giant screen, which offers a resolution that is rough compared even to mobile phone displays, poses a challenge to artists that use it as their medium. The work presented on the façade reexamines questions posed by the poorly received early computer art from the 1950s and 1970s as well as abstract and concrete art.

01

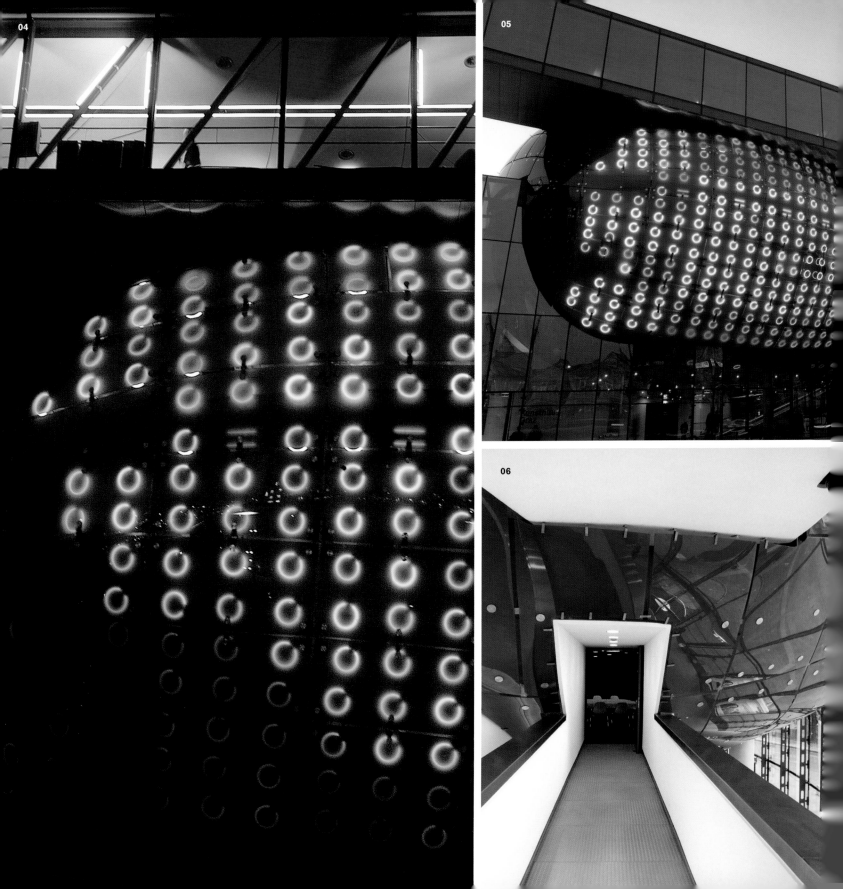

07

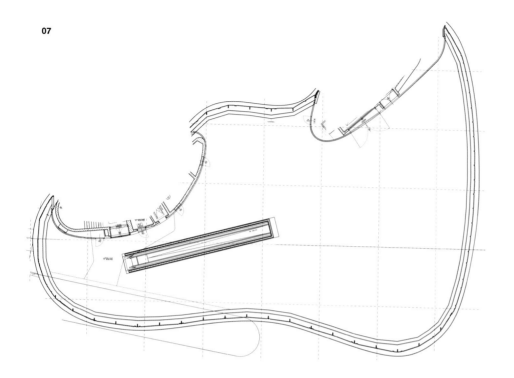

08

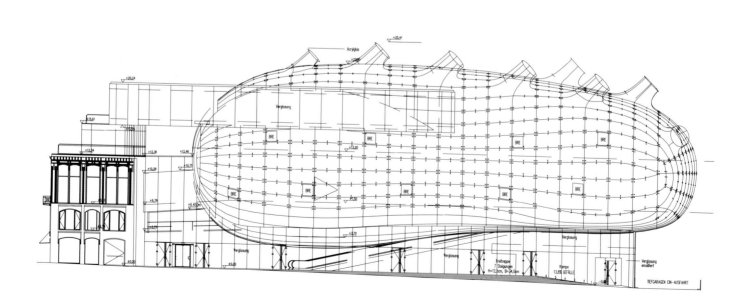

**Air Traffic Control Center with control tower, 2005
Address:** Towerstraße, Airport Vienna-Schwechat,
Austria. **Structural engineers:** Th. Lorenz. **Membrane
design:** Form TL. **Client:** Flughafen Wien AG – Austro
Control GmbH. **Gross floor area:** 8,600 m². **Materials:** steel, reinforced concrete, glass, membrane with
polytetrafluoroethylene (PTFE).

Five miles out
ARCHITECTS: Zechner & Zechner

The prominent location helped add a landmark quality to
the new tower standing at the main approach. A unique
identity with a signaling character has set the new technical structure apart from other towers. The base of the
building follows the curve of the street, while the head
is turned towards the runways. A membrane envelope is
stretched between, whose form was derived from stepwise "morphing" of these two contours. This irregular
shape demanded a material with extremely high specifications concerning fire resistance, absorption of highspeed winds, large-format laying for use as a projection
screen, and radar tolerance. The use of the membrane
as façade material required a special montage concept
in the shape of spanned rings strung up one after the
other. Depending on the light conditions, the membrane
can appear opaque. At night, interior illumination or projections from outside give the middle membrane panel
a more solid appearance, allowing it to develop a fullbodied character of its own.

04

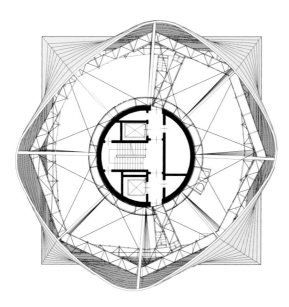

05

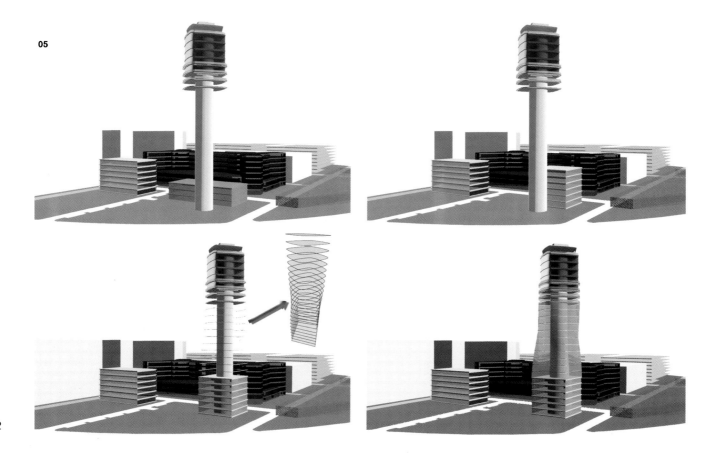

Front end D tower, 2004
Address: Grutstraat / Europaweg, Doetinchem, The Netherlands. **Artist:** Q. S. Serafijn. **Software:** V2_Lab. **Client:** City of Doetinchem. **Height:** 11.39 m. **Materials:** LEDs, polyepoxide (epoxy).

Stat(ist)ic

ARCHITECTS: NOX / Lars Spuybroek with Q. S. Serafijn

The cityscape of Doetinchem is to be enhanced with five art pieces portraying earth, water, light, time and fire. The tower presents the residents' emotions that are related to the idea of fire, but it is only one of three locations of the "fire project." The first is a "lifting of emotions" conducted daily via the Internet for registered residents. The second is the publicly viewable exhibit of the emoticon landscape in the Internet (www.d-toren.nl) and a corresponding forum. The 11.39 meter-high tower itself, whose form resembles a beating heart hung upside down, shows the emotion that currently predominates the city using integrated LEDs. Red symbolizes love, blue – happiness, yellow – fear, and green – hate. Nineteen glass fiber-reinforced epoxy parts formed by a computer-generated molding technique (CNC-milled Styrofoam) were glued together to create the tower itself. The walls are up to 4.5 mm thick and the tower has a weight of only 3,000 kg.

01 Emoticon landscape, color symbolizing happiness **02** Detail emoticon landscape, color symbolizing hate **03** Emoticon landscape, color symbolizing love

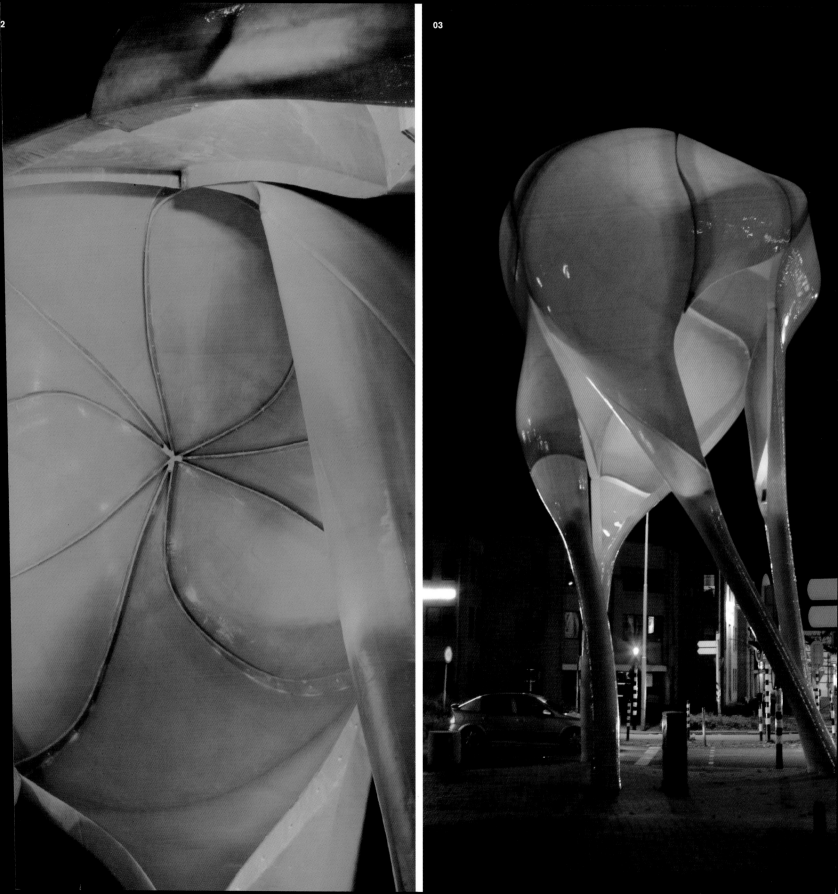

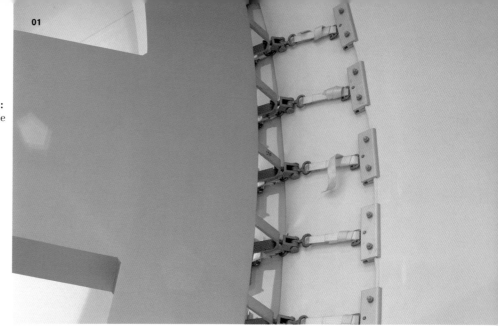

Trade fair pavilion Dynaform, 2001
Address: Frankfurt International Motor Show (IAA) 2001, Germany. **Client:** BMW Group. **Gross floor area:** 5,500 m². **Materials:** membane with polyvinyl chloride (PVC, "vinyl"), membrane with with polytetrafluoro-ethylene (PTFE).

Riding down the highwave

ARCHITECTS: Franken-Architekten

Despite the complexity of its form, Dynaform's façade appears reduced and minimalistic. The building enve-lope is devoid of an orthogonal grid or any details pro-viding a reference of scale. All protrusions are clearly detached from the skin of the building by ducts, and re-late to the orthogonality of the surroundings, and not to that of the structural form. As a free-standing sculpture, Dynaform defies all architectural categorization, and is therefore an object rather than a building. For the gen-eration of the Doppler Effect, a BMW 7 drives through a 3D matrix, linked by tubes. The superimposition of the context-related forces and the Doppler Effect pro-duces the Dynaform. The intricate shape is enveloped by a sheath made of PVC-covered glass fibers. Every section is twisted in two directions without any repeti-tions. The glass fibers perform the actual load-bearing role. The PVC layer acts as a mantle for climate con-trol, and has enough elasticity to sustain great changes in length during stretching. Dynaform's side openings, the gates, were realized using negative pressure mem-brane cushions from PTFE film that are drawn inside the structure.

02

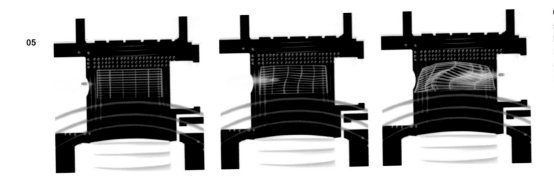

01 Detail skin **02** Construction side **03 + 04** BMW Group IAA 01 Dynaform **05** Generation of the Doppler Effect **06** Cross section **07** Membran of the Dynaform **08** Skin

06

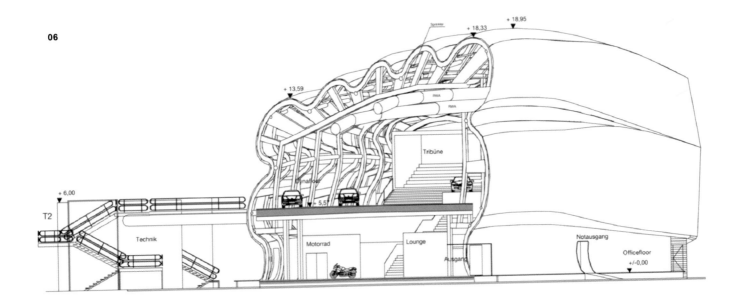

Het nieuwe Stedelijk Museum, 2009
Address: Paulus Potterstraat 13 – Museumplein, 1071 CX Amsterdam, The Netherlands. **Client:** City of Amsterdam. **Gross floor area:** 12,000 m². **Materials:** Tenax carbon fiber reinforced plastic (CFRP), Twaron p-phenylene terephtalamides (PPTA, aromatic polyamide, aramids) fibers.

The artist's tub

ARCHITECTS: Benthem Crouwel Architekten BV bna

The addition to the public museum creates a new main entrance on what up until now was the back façade of the structure on the Museumsplein. The late 19th century building has been preserved, and can be accessed via the glass ground story of the new addition. The new exposition space on the upper floors is located inside a plastic form that stretches with a projecting roof over the square. The new structure separates itself from the old museum not just through the use of different materials, but also through its asymmetrical assembly, while remaining inside the boundaries of the main building's silhouette. A yellow tube housing escalators transports visitors to the new floating rooms. This hovering "bath tub" with a surface measuring more than 3,000 m² is executed using a sandwich construction with eight layers of Twaron / Carbon hybrid fibers (350 g / m²). Twaron is a para-aramid (poly-paraphenylene terephthalamide), which is light, but five times stronger than steel, and exhibits no temperature-sensitive expansions or contractions. This allows the creation of a seamless façade. One of the industrial applications the material has found is in shipbuilding, where it is used for hulls.

01 Square **02** Exterior **03** Interior **04 + 05** Exterior

Kreipe's coffeeshop lounge, 2004
Address: Rathenaustraße 12, Hanover, Germany. **Client:** Konditorei Kreipe GmbH / Jan Fleissig. **Gross floor area:** 250 m². **Materials:** black medium density fiberboard, DLW-Vinyl polyvinyl chloride (PVC, "vinyl"), woven polyvinyl chloride (PVC, "vinyl").

Vinyl cremissimo

ARCHITECTS: Despang Architekten

The traditional coffee shop commissioned a branch to be built specifically for a new target group. On the ground floor, linear decorative elements guide the guest inside the space. Seating and counters are not free-standing, but emerge smoothly, complete with all their components from the light-colored plastic that makes up the floor. This allows their mass to dissolve, and lets the forms define the space. The furniture is covered with a 2 mm-thick crème vinyl layer. This is DLW Solid, which is the coating covering all faces. Authentic materials that display their composition on open surfaces are the basic elements of the design concept. Pre-patinated, banded brass elements were employed on tables and the buffet, transporting the coffeehouse tradition into the modern age. The sensual harmony arising from the combination of plastic and brass is a reference to the Copenhagen Airport Terminal designed by Vilhelm Lauritzen (1935). The vinyl used on the ground floor, with its smooth, hard surface is a perfect match for the quick coffee experience. On the upper floor it is replaced with a woven texture reminiscent of textile that covers the floor, seating and the first two meters of the lounge ceiling, formulating the space here as well.

04

PVC-Verlegung Übergang
Fußboden - Tresen

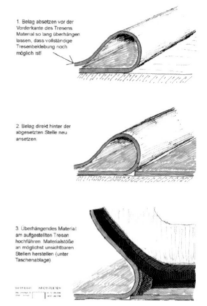

1. Belag absetzen vor der
Vorderkante des Tresens
Material so lang überhängen
lassen, dass vollständige
Tresenbeklebung noch
möglich ist!

2. Belag direkt hinter der
abgesetzten Stelle neu
ansetzen.

3. Überhängendes Material
am aufgestellten Tresen
hochführen Materialstöße
an möglichst unsichtbaren
Stellen herstellen (unter
Taschenablage).

05

01 Detail bar **02** Buffet **03** Lounge
on the upper floor **04** Detail floor
construction **05** Detail **06** Ground
floor plan **07** Seating and counters
in the entrance area

06

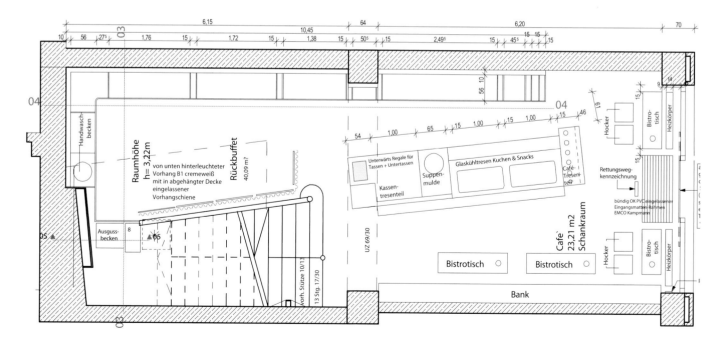

156

Bizarre Boutique, 2005
Address: 17255 Davenport, Suite 101, Omaha, NE 68118, USA. **Client:** Djel Brown. **Gross floor area:** 150 m². **Materials:** hollow metal (frames), painted high density particle board, Lithochrome Cementone Clear Sealer (floor), painted drywall (walls), metal studs, clear, tempered glass (shelving), Vistawall system (storefront), milky white polymethyl methacrylate (PMMA, "acrylic glass"; acrylic).

Female curves

ARCHITECTS: Randy Brown Architects

A women's boutique was the perfect opportunity to challenge the typical retail store conventions where the walls, fixtures, ceilings, and floors are all separate elements. It also provided a chance to test processes of blending these elements to generate space where the store itself becomes the podium to display the merchandise as art objects. The solution was to fabricate a continuous surface to lead you into the space and to define it. This surface bends, folds and is cut to display merchandise and conceal mechanics, creating a visually pure backdrop for a memorable shopping experience. Molded plastic played an important role in the forming of the reception desk and the exterior forms. The display shelves are also a "plastic form" constructed from drywall. Plastic was utilized based on the fact that it provides a sturdy base for the curved forms. Nebraska weather being so unpredictable, it was also used for the exterior due to its weather resistance qualities.

04

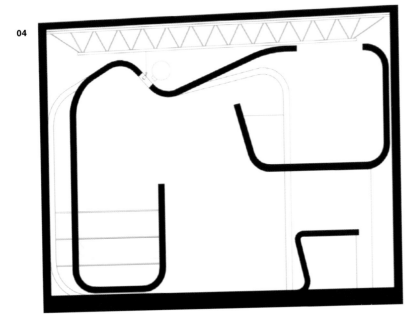

05

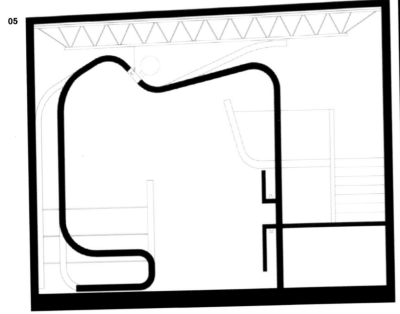

06

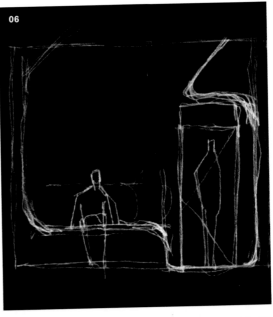

07

Public space city lounge St. Gallen, 2005
Address: Vadianstrasse, Schreinerstrasse, Garten-
strasse and Kornhausstrasse, St. Gallen, Switzerland.
Client: City of St. Gallen & Verband der Raiffeisen-
bank. **Gross floor area:** 4,400 m². **Materials:** traffic
signs, trees, hydrocarbon polymer granulated rubber.

Paint the town red

ARCHITECTS: Carlos Martinez and Pipilotti Rist

The newly-designed Raiffeisen complex, located on
what used to be a falling apart collection of open space
and traffic routing structures, was charged with bringing
the area together into one whole. The space should become an inviting place continuous with the central pedestrian zone. All plazas, empty spaces and traffic surfaces were united into a public "lounge" using fire-alarm
red, unusually soft floor covering made of rubber granu-
late. The homely, pleasant to the touch carpeting also
covers all free-standing furniture elements like seating,
benches and tables like a large drape. The relationship
between outer and inner space is reversed and breaks
our usual visual associations with public space, forming
an optical blur at the border between leisure, pedestrian
and traffic areas. The affixed signs give the impression
that they are only temporarily placed exhibition pieces.
The greenery that includes four large gingko trees, and
lights with abstract shapes filling out the top of the
space, complete the production.

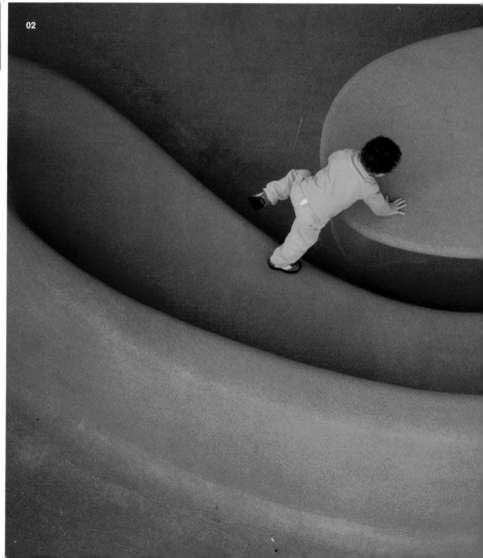

07

01 Detail soft floor made of granulated rubber **02** Everything is covered with the flooring **03** Furnishing elements **04** Lounging on the square **05** Detail material **06** Bird's eye view **07** Sketch **08** Site plan **09** Sketch

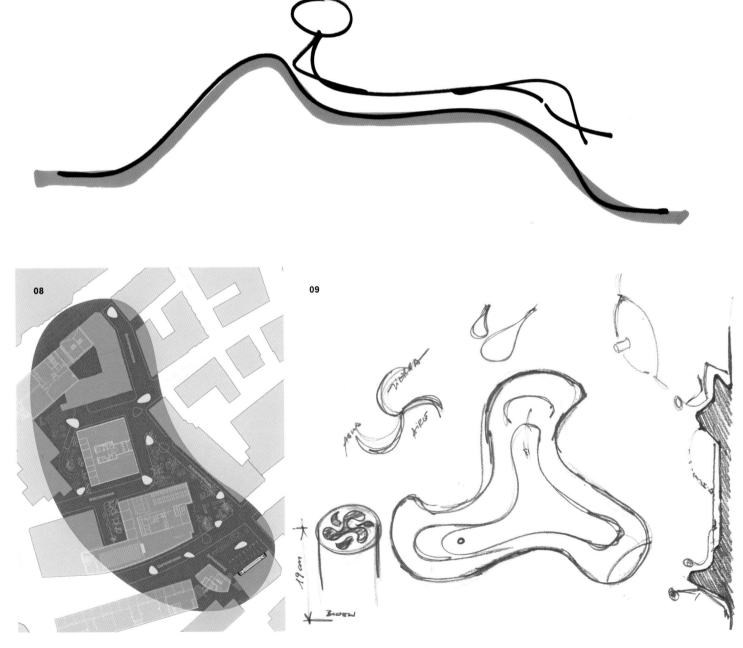

08

09

Caravan Adria Action, 2005
Realisation and production: Adria Mobil d.o.o. **Client:** Adria Mobil d.o.o. **Gross floor area:** up to 7.5 m².
Materials: glass-reinforced polyester (GRP).

Keep it rolling

IDEA: Reimo, DESIGN: Nina Mihovec

The designer, who received Slovenia's "Designer of the Year" award for this work, has examined the idea of the minimal apartment. She follows the tradition of Le Corbusier, who saw ship quarters as functionally complete. The swinging rear optically underlines the caravan's dynamic, creating an instantly recognizable shape. All other forms are also characterized by round edges. This optical expression and small size (capacity for three persons) makes the caravan attractive for young, design-conscious audience who is also interested in vanity car brands like the Smart, Beetle or Mini. The plastic structure with colors blue and silver reduces the total weight of the camping wagon's weight to 800 kg.

05

01 Front **02** Kitchen **03** Interior
04 Exterior **05** Isometry **06** Floor
plan **07** Caravan Adria on a camping ground

06

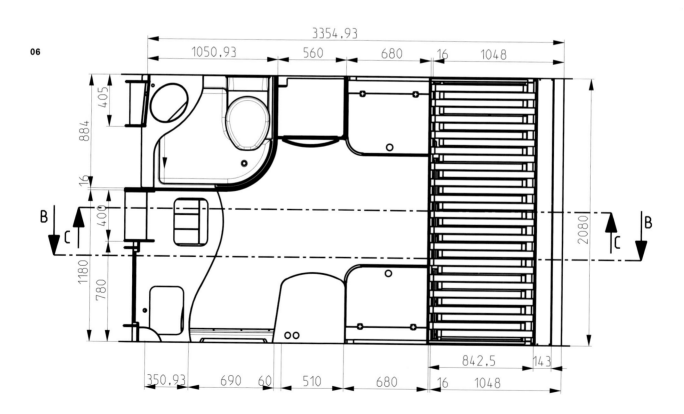

Hydra saltwater pavilion, 1997
Address: Neeltje Jans-Island, Burgh-Haamstede, The Netherlands. **Sound environment:** Edwin van der Heide, Victor Wentinck. **Project architect:** Kas Oosterhuis. **Design team body and design real time behaviour:** Kas Oosterhuis, Menno Rubbens. **Design team hydra:** Kas Oosterhuis, Ilona Lénárd, Menno Rubbens. **Design virtual worlds:** Kas Oosterhuis, Menno Rubbens, Károly Tóth. **Composers:** Edwin van der Heide, Victor Wentinck. **Sensors:** Bert Bongers. **Client:** Stichting Delta Expo Eiland Neeltje Jans. **Gross floor area:** 1,050 m². **Materials:** metal structure, polycarbonate (PC), fiber-reinforced polymer (FRP, "glass fiber").

Aquaplan(n)ing
ARCHITECTS: ONL [Oosterhuis_Lénárd]

The sand shore was originally built as a storm surge barrier in the Oosterschelde, and was expanded to serve as the basis for Neeltje Jans' work. After the project was finished, an exhibit about salt water (NOX / Lars Spuybroek) and freshwater examining all their forms and elements took place here. The flowing architecture matches to the theme. The interior consists of two areas horizontally divided using a wave floor. The bottom area, the Wet Lab, is a dark and moist environment filled with water, the amounts of which depend on tidal movements of the sea. A panorama window in the upper area, the Sensorium, is blocked or opened by an inflatable object and reveals virtual representations of water. Multi-colored fiber optic cables and a system of active speakers are lodged in the Wet Lab's water and the walls of the upper story. They are controlled by a central computer using pre-programmed algorithms, and react to visitors and changing environmental conditions.

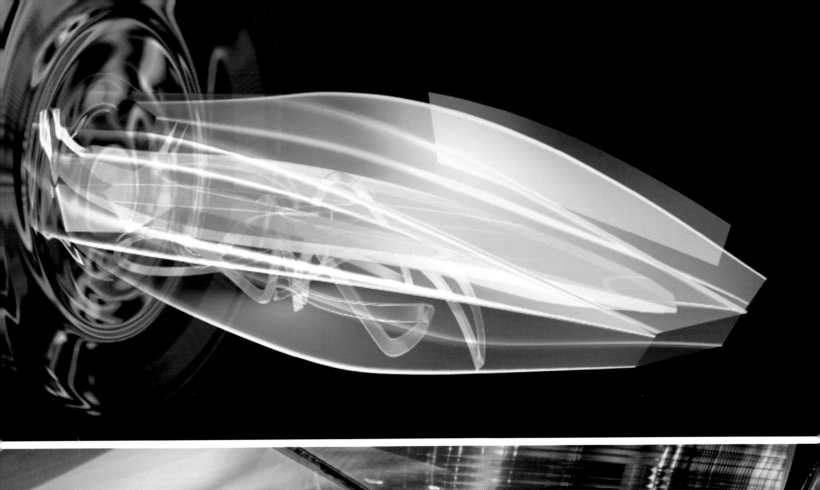
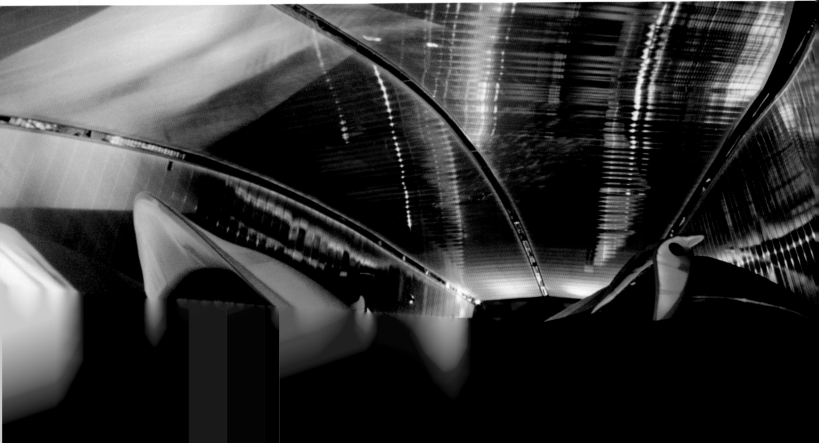

05

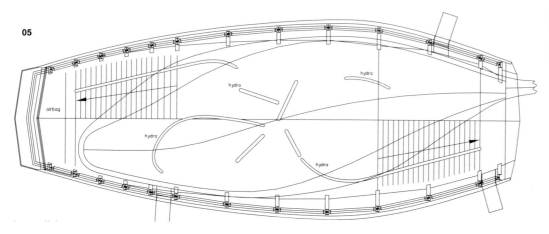

06

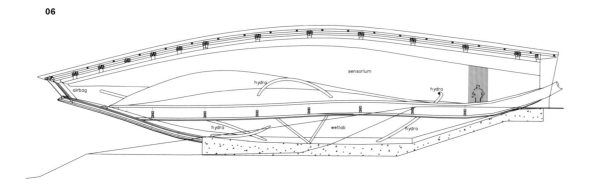

07

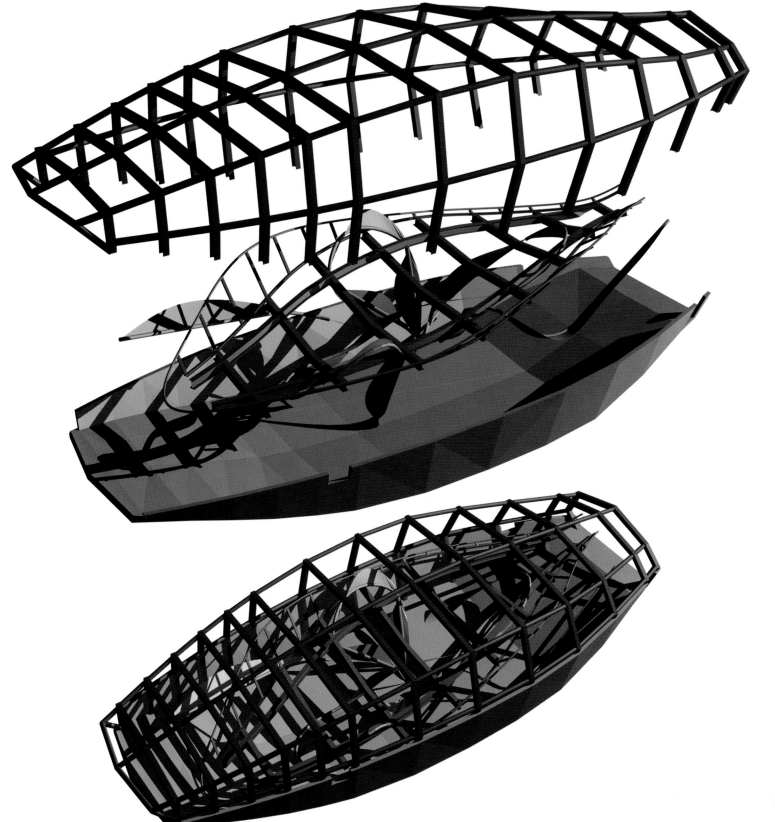

Office and presentation building, terminal V, 2000
Address: Wolfurterstraße 15, 6932 Lauterach, Austria.
Fiberglass façade elements: Swiss shielding Corporation. **Client:** Hefel Wohnbau AG. **Gross floor area:** 1,800 m². **Materials:** steel, reinforced concrete, fiber-reinforced polymer (FRP, fiber-reinforced plastic), carbon fiber reinforced plastic (CFRP), foam made of polyurethane (PU).

Shift control

ARCHITECTS: Hugo Dworzak

The company located in a residential building not only wanted to expand its office space but, more importantly, needed a multimedia presentation room for 3D animations of their structural projects. The room, where the presentation of the non-contextual "No place" (Marc Augé) could be viewed, is a middle ground between reality and virtual space. Already when entering this connecting space, a transferal of the architectural medium from reality into simulated reality should occur. A similar effect happens upon boarding a plane, whereby the passengers enter a simulated, introverted world. The formal design of the 3D presentation room is completed with images from airplane construction, but in conforming to its internal functions, it is correspondingly altered. The multi-leaf wall structure, displaced in relation to itself (fiberglass outside, translucent plastic foil inside) makes possible the indirect addition of natural or artificial light, and with it, adjustable amounts of reality alteration.

01 Exterior view from south **02** Entrance **03** Exterior view from east
04 Sections **05** First floor plan **06**
Presentation room

04

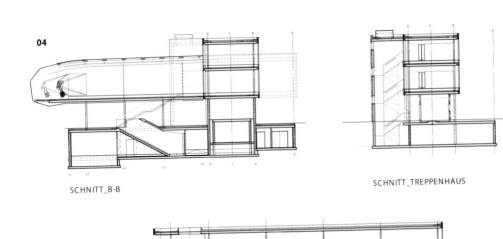

SCHNITT_B-B   SCHNITT_TREPPENHAUS

SCHNITT A-A

05

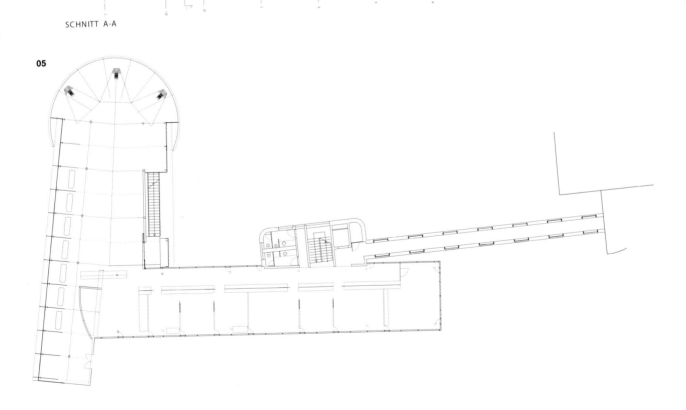

Terminal V

**Bus station "The Amazing Whale Jaw", 2003
Address:** Spaarneziekenhuis, Hoofddorp, The Netherlands. **Client:** Schiphol Project Consult. **Gross floor area:** 338 m². **Materials:** polyethylene terephthalate (PET, "polyester"; surface), polystyrene (PS, polystyrol; core).

Peter-Paul's fish

ARCHITECTS: NIO Architecten

The bus station is located in the middle of a square, and is a public space in the form of an island that functions as a local bus service hub. The design of this kind of building is generally neutral, but here the aim was to create a strong, individual image that was less austere and generic. Hence, the building was designed in the tradition of Oscar Niemeyer as a synthesis between white Modernism and black Baroque. The available budget precluded conventional construction methods. The use of synthetic materials allowed the architects to produce a Rubenesque form without the downsides that come with using concrete and steel. The building is made completely of polystyrene foam and polyester and is, as such, the world's largest synthetic materials structure (50 x 10 x 5 m). People often wonder about the building's shape and what it represents, and there are a number of possible answers. All of these are simultaneously correct and irrelevant. Like the white face of a geisha, every opinion and image can be projected onto the building, which has no answers of its own. After some time, the building received a makeover in orange.

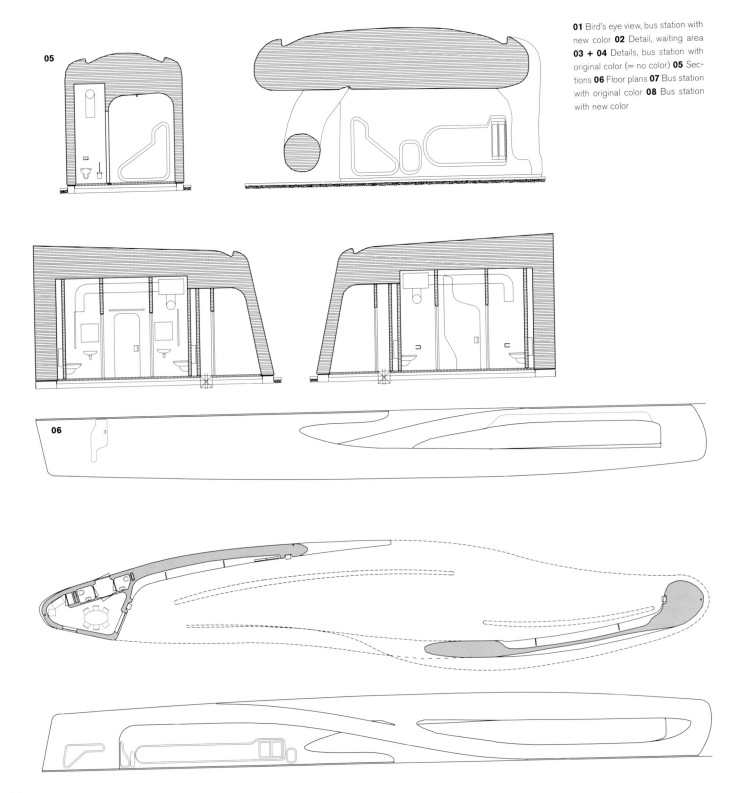

05

01 Bird's eye view, bus station with new color **02** Detail, waiting area **03 + 04** Details, bus station with original color (= no color) **05** Sections **06** Floor plans **07** Bus station with original color **08** Bus station with new color

06

180

01

Heat Transfer Station Nr. 8 Zero emission, 1998
Address: Rijkstraatweg 12a, Utrecht, The Netherlands.
Structural engineers: DHV AIB BV. **Clients specialist:** ir. Djin Sie. **Client:** Energy production company
UNA N.V. Bureau Nieuwbouw Centrales. **Materials:**
polyurethane (PU).

A Dutch mountain
ARCHITECTS: NL Architects

The heat transfer station (WOS 8) was built for the new
city of Leidsche Rijn, an extension of Utrecht. The cooling water of the UNA power plant, a kilometer away,
has enough energy to supply all new dwellings (11,000)
with heat and warm water. WOS 8 is the junction where
the loop from the power plant transfers its energy to
several distribution loops. At the moment, WOS 8 is
located behind a picturesque farm, while later it found
itself situated in the middle of a contemporary suburban
idyll. The size of WOS 8 is determined by its minimal
functional dimensions. It is architecture reduced to a
designed skin. A membrane of polyurethane enables
architecture to become seamless. The material was
originally developed for parking roofs: strong, flexible,
waterproof, durable, attractive and chemically inert (no
pollution of earth and ground water). The façade is programmed with a number of activities that intend to make
the building attractive, like a public square wrapped
around a box. The climbing grips applied in Braille spell
a message "the blind façade".

02

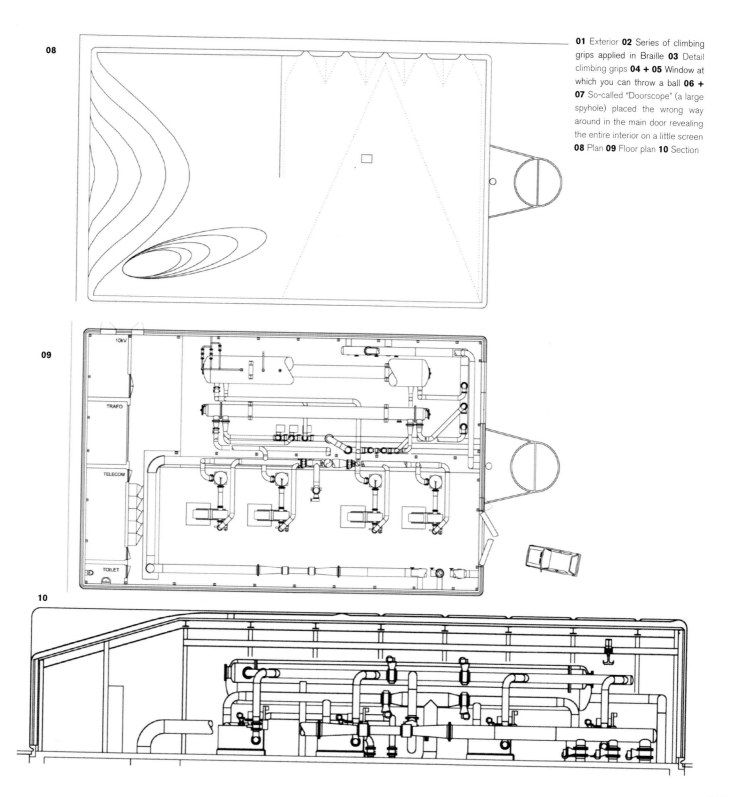

01 Exterior **02** Series of climbing grips applied in Braille **03** Detail climbing grips **04 + 05** Window at which you can throw a ball **06 + 07** So-called "Doorscope" (a large spyhole) placed the wrong way around in the main door revealing the entire interior on a little screen **08** Plan **09** Floor plan **10** Section

08

09

10kV

TRAFO

TELECOM

TOILET

10

Restaurant Georges, 2000
Address: Centre Georges Pompidou, Paris, France.
Client: Costes. **Gross floor area:** 1,400 m². **Materials:**
aluminum, modular plastic chairs, Vibrasto (synthetic-
chemical textile fibers, foam made of polyurethane (PU)).

Parasites under the floor
ARCHITECTS: JAKOB + MACFARLANE

The restaurant located on the sixth floor of the Centre Georges Pompidou had to create an appropriate
response inside such a unique architectural context.
The architects decided to leave the space as it was and
make their intervention as light as possible. The concept
was that of inserting new elements just by sliding volumes – kitchen, bar, coat check, private reception room,
private dining space. Under the reshaped floor, a new
landscape of both interior and exterior conditions was
created. The floor surface, or "skin," was made out of
aluminum, a material which when burnished, both ab-
sorbs and reflects light. This effect reinforces the notion
of background, of appearance and disappearance. The
volumes find their eventual form and position through
the usual negotiation process of design, frozen in a
state of movement. The space pockets are coated inside with red, green, yellow and orange Vibrasto. The
space "taps into" the building grid of the Pompidou
center, and the "host" provides all fluids to the pockets
though the ceiling.

01 Restaurant Georges **02–04** Details

Khan Shatyry Entertainment Center, 2008
Address: Astana, Kazakhstan. **Co-architects:** Linea Tusavul Architecture, Gultekin Architecture. **Client:** Sembol Construction. **Gross floor area:** 100,000 m².
Materials: Polyethylene terephthalate (PET, "polyester"), polytetrafluoroethylene (PTFE).

My tent is my city

ARCHITECTS: Foster + Partners

The Khan Shatyry, the "Royal Marquee" rises from a 200 meters elliptical base to form the highest peak on the skyline of Astana. Kisho Kurikawa created the urban plan of the city. Norman Foster had already built a glass-and-steel pyramid here, the Palace of Peace and Reconciliation. The new "tent" houses a complete city with squares and streets, an urban-scale park, a shopping and entertainment venue with restaurants and a cinema, a concert hall with 5,000 seats, a boating river, a mini golf and an indoor beach resort. The highest terrace is a viewing deck which will offer dramatic views over the park. From a tower whose height reaches 150 meters, a transparent EFTE membrane with a total length of 40 kilometers and weighing 1.2 tons is suspended using a rope system. The ETFE polymer weighs only 1% of the mass of glass and stretches to three times its normal length without losing its elasticity. While year round outside temperatures vary from -35 to +35°C, ETFT allows sunlight which, in conjunction with air heating and cooling systems, maintain an internal temperature between 15–30°C in the main space and 19–24°C in the retail units.

01 Section **02** Bird's eye view **03** Exterior by day **04** Exterior by night

02

3

**MANDARING! Mandarina Duck Agency shop, 2002
Address:** differing. **Client:** Mandarina Duck. **Materials:** wood, aluminum, steel, glass, ceramic slabs, high pressure laminates (HPL, coated wood panels, "laminate"), polymethyl methacrylate (PMMA, "acrylic glass").

Glowing cave

ARCHITECTS: Studio X Design Group (STX): Rettondini+Brito

The project for Mandarina Duck Agency shops has been developed according to the strategy of distribution. The initial brief asked for a proposal that would have a strong impact and be able to update the existing store image while preserving its shelf structure. In addition to these conditions the project was required to be built on a low budget and fitted in a very short time. As a response to these requests, STX developed a project that avoids fragmentation that results from spreading furniture pieces around the shop. A single cohesive structure, on the contrary, reflects brand values in a plastic and playful, while functional totality. The shops are almost identical, put together using different "Mandarings" – yellow modules that originate in a continuous surface linking floor, walls, ceiling and including shop display elements; the objects' shapes are transformed into the final structures like tables, pedestals, benches, vertical displays, or even lamps and showcases that come down from the ceiling like stalactites. The modular concept ensures uniformity of the shops' image around the world on the one hand, while creating unique spaces on the other.

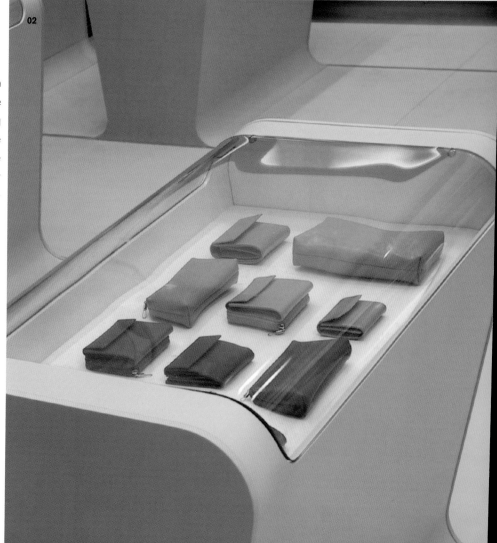

04

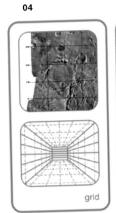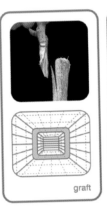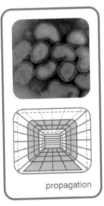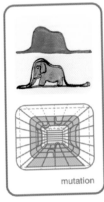

grid　　graft　　propagation　　mutation　　transition

01 Mandarina Duck Agency shop in Paris **02** Shop display elements **03** Central furniture with the external surface covered with yellow laminate, and the interior surfaces covered with white laminate **04** Concept **05** Cohesion **06** Section A **07** Floor plan Mandarina Duck Agency shop in Paris **08** Showcase coming down from the ceiling like a stalactite

05

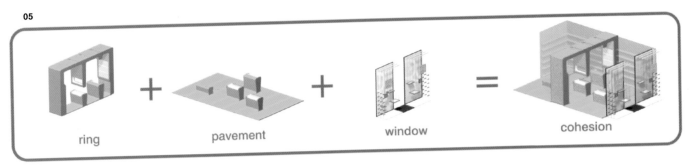

ring　　+　　pavement　　+　　window　　=　　cohesion

06

07

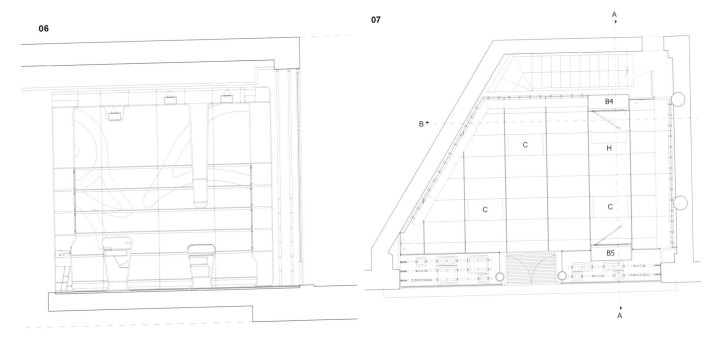

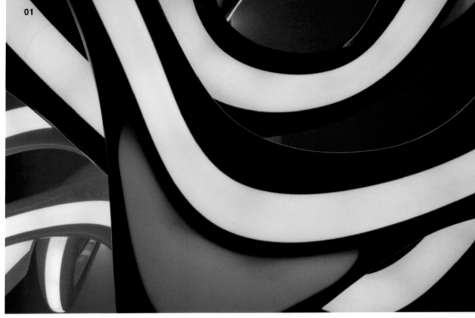

Ideal houses, 2007
Address: IMM international furniture fair, Cologne, Germany. **Client:** Koelnmesse. **Gross floor area:** 200 m².
Materials: metal, wood, polystyrene (PS, polystyrol), polyurethane (PU).

Expanding capacity

ARCHITECTS: Zaha Hadid Architects

The eye-catching red cubes are a trademark feature of Cologne's international furniture fair. Innovative designers can use them to realize their visions of future living space. In Hadid's ideal house rooms lose all orthogonality, and come together not as cubes, but stretch out inside the cube as asymmetrical space bubbles, erasing it along the edges and in corners. As in a group of soap bubbles, the closed volume of space, not the skin, determines the material's staying in the shape of surfaces and bridges. All the same, the stretching of space is not determined by physical laws, but guided by the designer's will, function and abstraction. For modeling of the rounded edges on the metal frame, 400 m³ of polystyrene were used. The continuous surface received a coating of 1.8 tons polyurethane.

AQUA TABLE 2005
E ESTABLISHED & SONS

08

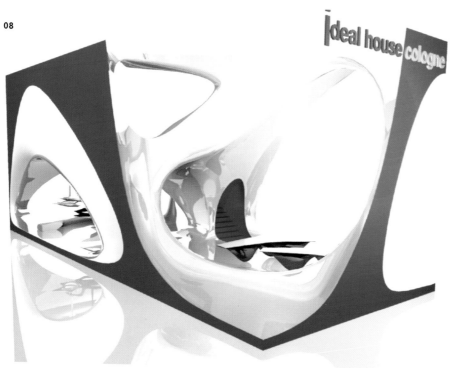

ideal house cologne

09

ideal house cologne

Temporary Museum, unrealized
Address: Schlossplatz, Berlin, Germany. **Client:** City of Berlin. **Materials:** wood, steel, ethylene tetrafluoro-ethylene (ETFE).

Stadtterrasse Kabinette semitransparente, wetterfeste Medienmembran

Zwischenzone:
öffentliches Raumtragwerk

Ausstellungshalle

landschaftliche Sockelzone:
Kasse, Café, Museumsshop, Verwaltung, Lager

SCHNITTPERSPEKTIVE

Cloud 9
ARCHITECTS: Graft

The airy, dynamic form of this proposal for a temporary structure to be built on Berlin's Schlossplatz (Castle Square), clearly separates itself from the surrounding structures, including earlier buildings designed by Karl Friedrich Schinkel, the dismantled Palace of the Republic from the GDR and the reconstruction of the Prussian Castle planned for the future. The redesign of this historical place had led to much controversy concerning reconstructing historicism in general and its political statement in particular. Similarly to Christo's draping of the Reichstag, a completely independent visual experience should be created here as a symbol of a new beginning. An ethereal cloud is to float above a base zone encased in wood which, while remaining a self-sufficient form, should be the deflection point for the surrounding traffic routing zones and various elevations of the square. The cloud is made using space-filling framework with pneumatically-supported ETFE foil pillows. Air pressure variation in the graphically ornamented pillows allows flexible sun screening solutions, while the air filling serves as thermo isolation, too.

01 Section **02** Museum with exterior staircase **03** Roof terrace **04** Exterior by night

02

Piece of furniture, place of seclusion, AVL Work-skull, 2005
Address: changing. **Client:** no, produced in collaboration with Lensvelt B.V. **Dimensions:** 150 x 150 x 165 cm. **Materials:** wood, polyethylene terephthalate (PET, "polyester").

It's in your head

ARCHITECTS: Atelier Van Lieshout

The artist collective Atelier Van Lieshout (AVL), founded by the Dutch artist Joep van Lieshout in 1995, gained international recognition because of their stunning works such as mobile homes and functional sculptures. AVL Workskull is a typical example of such a piece of functional art. The skull, often featured in artists' work, is represented here quite abstractly, and can be recognized only by its silhouette and eye holes. AVL Workskull was designed as a secluded space in a large office where employees can work alone undisturbed, have more privacy for phone calls or retreat from the world. There are many reasons why Joep van Lieshout chooses to work with polyester: The material is durable and water resistant, making it very practical, it is artificial and minimal, but at the same time has a warm feel, and it is clean and hygienic. In addition, it suits the sometimes controversial subjects AVL touches.

01 The AVL Workskull in the forest **02** Entrance **03** Exterior

**Fair stand for EgoKiefer Windows and Doors,
2005 / 2007**
Address: Swissbau trade fair, Basel, Switzerland.
Client: EgoKiefer. **Gross floor area:** 448 m². **Materials:** colored polymethyl methacrylate (PMMA, "acrylic glass").

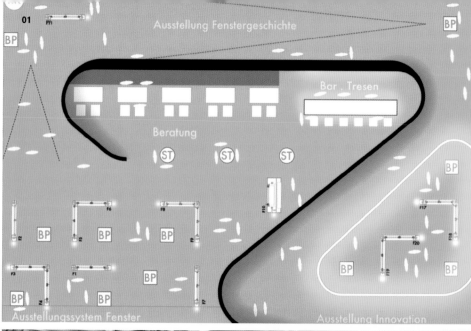

Leaving the door open

ARCHITECTS: Carlos Martinez Architekten

The trade fair stand is entered by climbing a step which acts as a large pedestal, similar to a theatrical stage, presenting a wall-less space for doors and windows. The rest of the stand is built as a fitting continuum, creating a flowing spatial experience of atmospheres, interactions, surprises, impressions conveyed using light, color, music and video. Instead of sealing off, opening up of space is the main theme of the windows and doors on view. Transition from the lower to the upper level is achieved using a ramp that integrates the visitor's entire track around the exhibit, allowing views of the stand and the entire trade fair that change with every step. The hierarchy reduction is a significant psychological aspect of the structure's effect on the public.

01 Floor plan **02** Trade fair stand **03** Bar **04** Meeting area

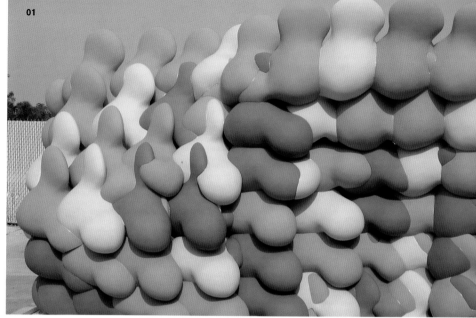

01

BlobWall©, 2007
Address: anywhere. **Co-development and production:** Panelite. **Robotic cutting technology:** Machineous. **Client:** Panelite. **Gross floor area:** undefined.
Materials: linear low density polyethylene (LLDPE).

To blob in layers

ARCHITECTS: Greg Lynn Form

BlobWall© is an innovative redefinition of architecture's most basic building unit, the brick; in lightweight, plastic, colorful, modular elements custom shaped using the latest CNC technology. It is a free-standing, indoor / outdoor wall system built of a low-density, recyclable, impact-resistant polymer. The blob unit, or "brick," is a tri-lobed hollow shape that is mass produced through rotational molding. Each wall is assembled from individually robotically cut hollow bricks that interlock with exacting precision. In addition to stock designs, custom configurations are available for specific shapes, sizes, room configurations, partitions and color schemes. The contemporary wall system that recovers the voluptuous shapes, chiaroscuro and grotto like textures of baroque and renaissance architecture in pixilated gradients of vivid color for a variety of residential and commercial applications.

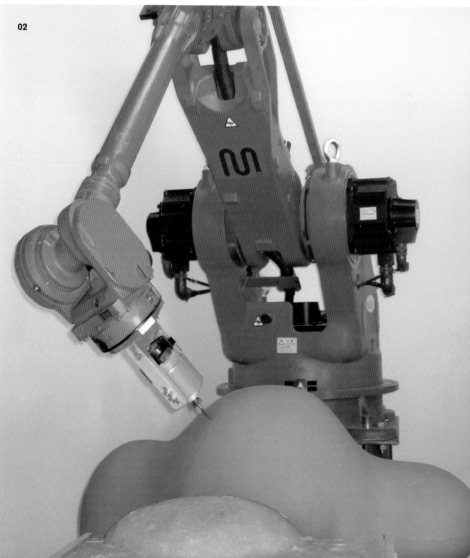

02

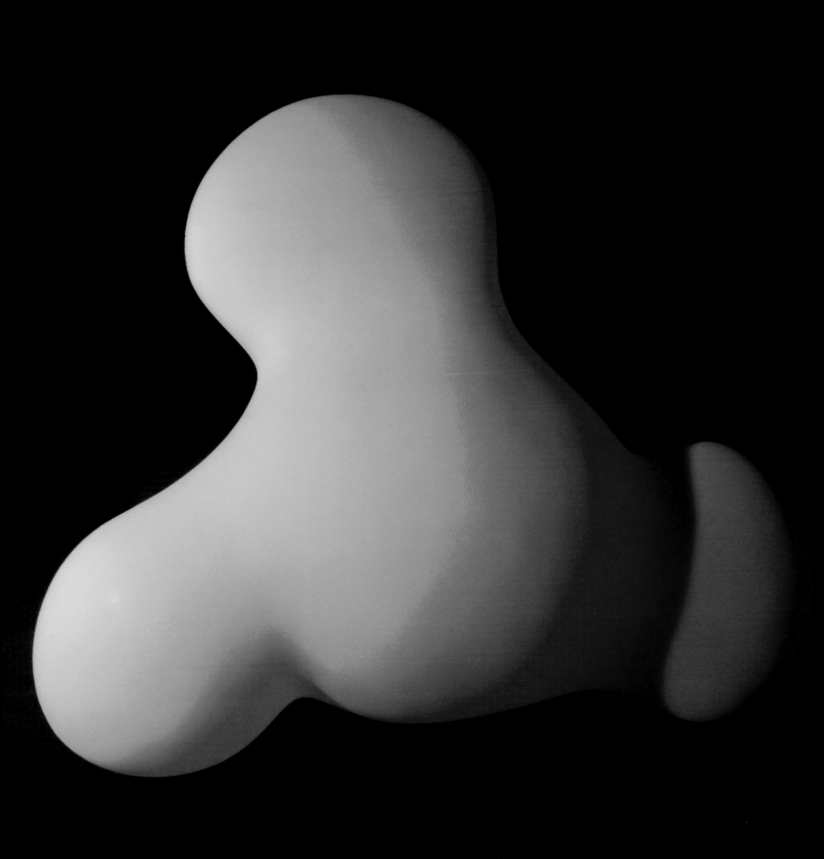

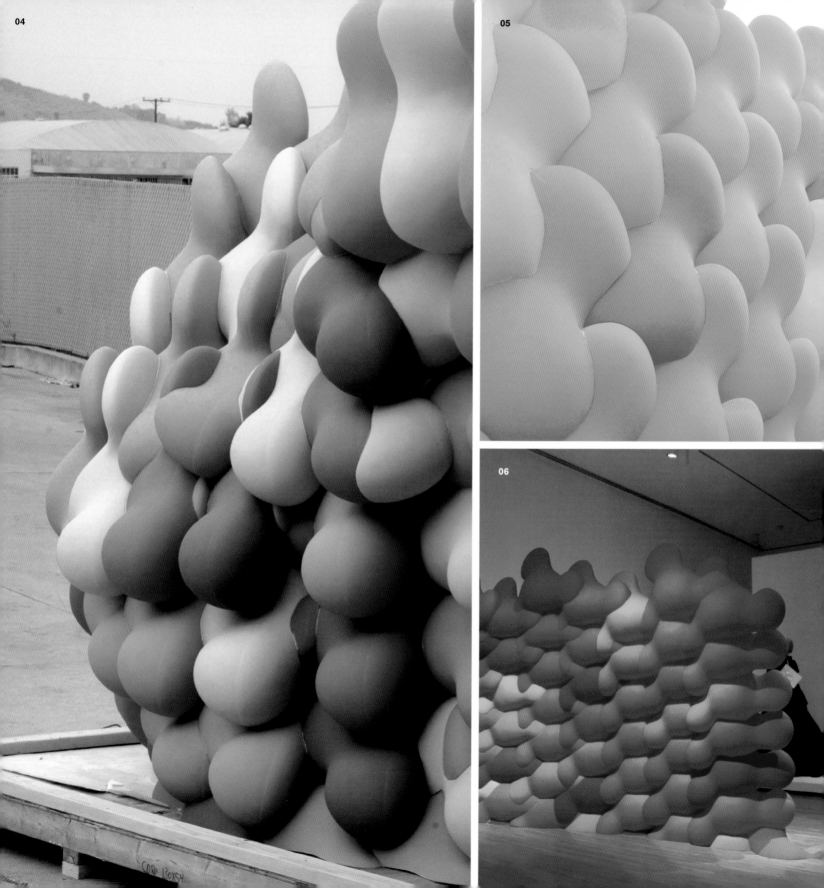

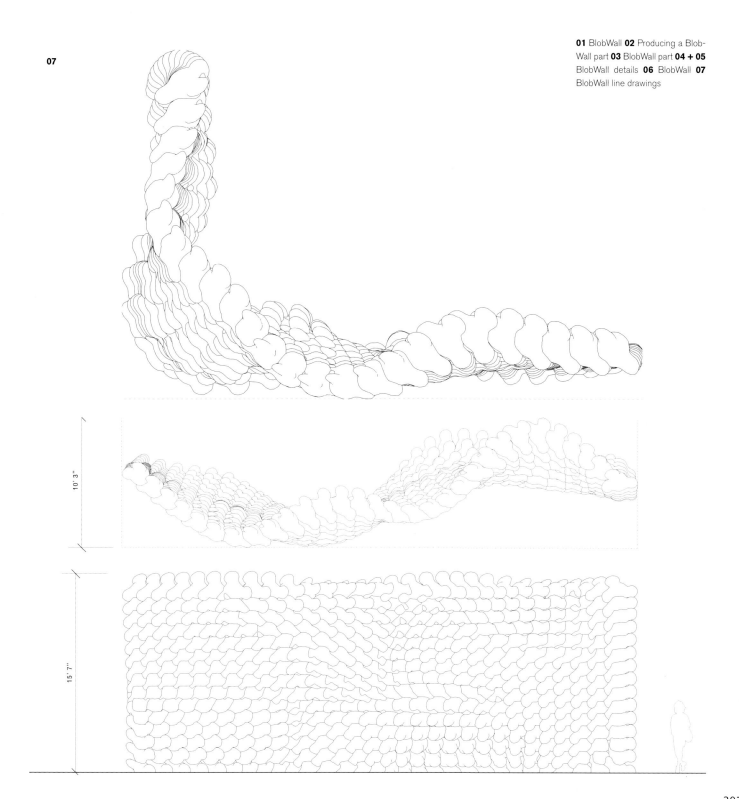

10' 3"

15' 7"

HYPER

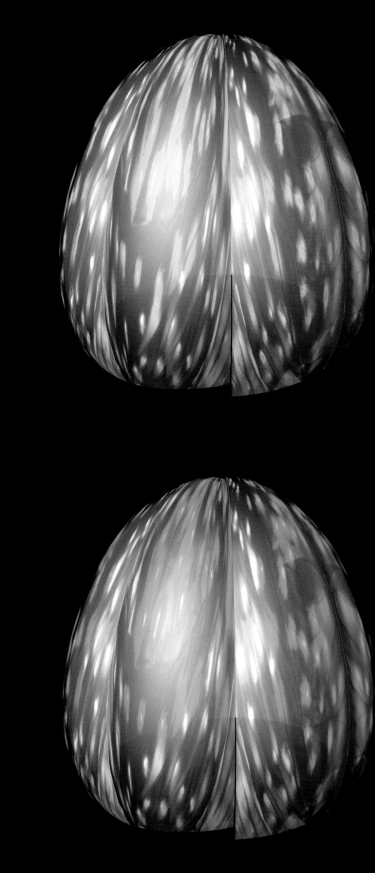

**Experimental construction CORPFORM, 2006
Address:** Vitra Design Museum, Weil am Rhein, Germany. **Client:** Vitra Design Stiftung gGmbH. **Structural engineers:** Teuffel Engineering. **Gross floor area:** 4.5 m². **Materials:** phase change materials (PCM, alkane hydrocarbons).

Heart chamber

ARCHITECTS: FORMORF (Marco Hemmerling, Markus Holzbach)

The CORPFORM project is meant to demonstrate analogies to living organisms. Using chemical and / or physical modifications, the building's envelope and structure can adapt to changing climate and weather conditions. Opaqueness, maintained temperature as well as ventilation, acoustics and color properties, not to mention the overall form can all be manipulated. The pneumatic load-carrying construction contracts and relaxes, during which the fragile glass fiber structure takes over the support function. Reservoir pads are built into the load carrying structure, which activate thermal mass. A Phase Change Material (PCM) is a substance with a high heat of fusion which, melting and solidifying at certain temperatures, is capable of storing or releasing large amounts of energy. It is incorporated into these pads, which can change their aggregate state and to save heat energy, releasing it slowly over time. A textile membrane with a ceramic layer serves an isothermal function; this is technology originally developed for the aeronautics and space travel industry. The constantly changing illumination, that is created by a layer of over 300 glass fiber strands, visualizes the adaptive properties of the experimental structure.

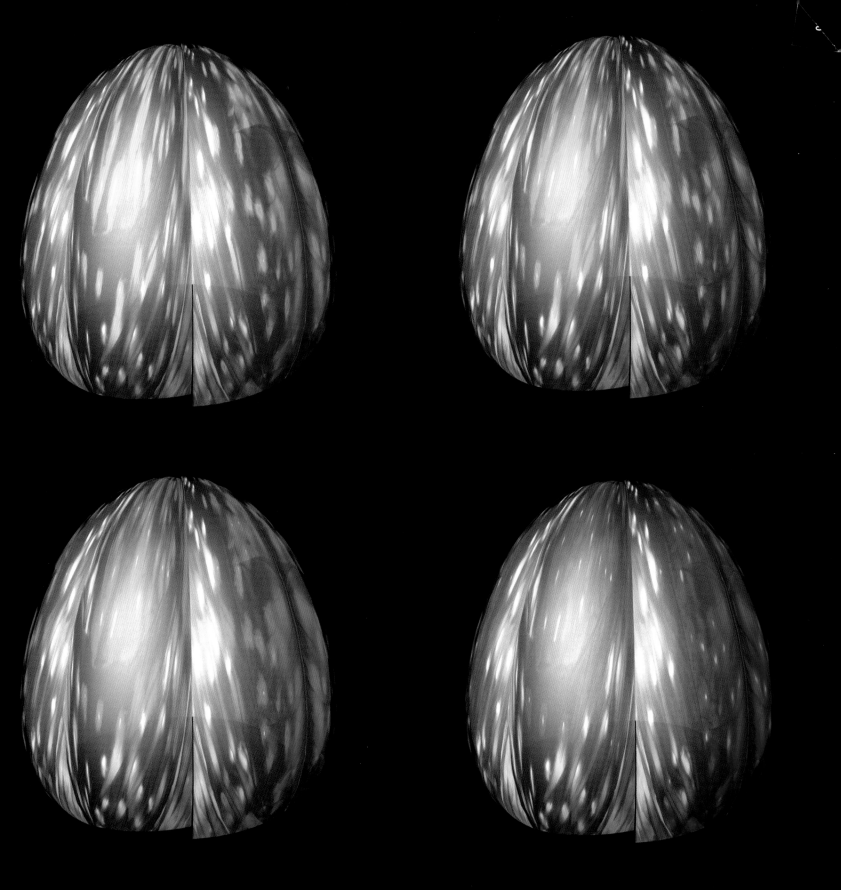

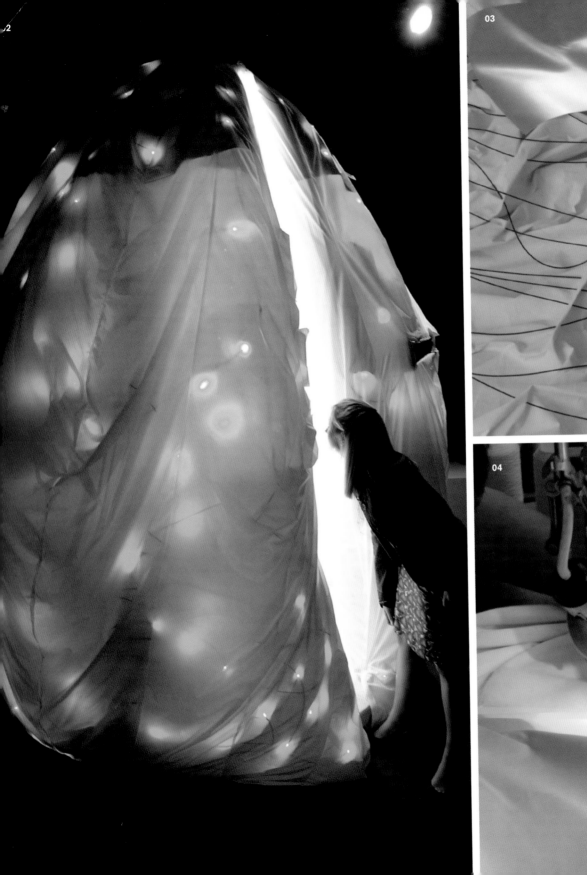

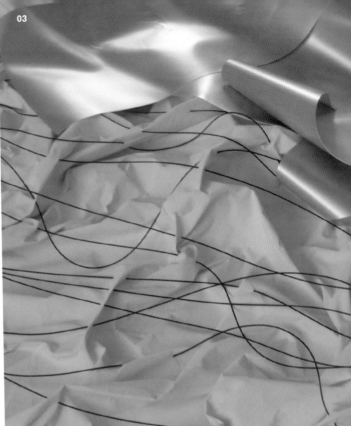

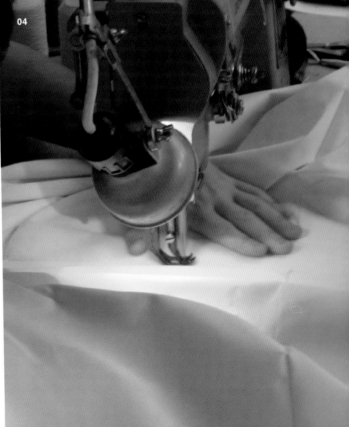

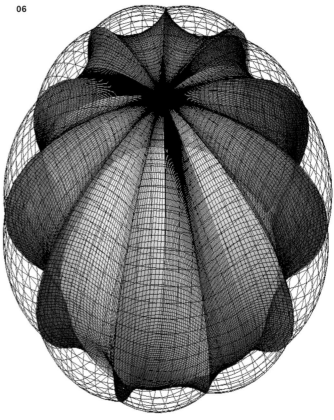

01 Renderings of the illumination concept **02** CORPFORM on the Entry 2006 in Essen **03** Different material layers **04** Sewing process of the functional layers **05** Construction outside **06** Construction inside

01

Tea Room: Tee Haus, 2005
Address: Schaumainkai 17, Frankfurt / Main, Germany. **Structural engineers:** Form TL GmbH, Taiyo Europe GmbH. **Client:** Museum für Angewandte Kunst Frankfurt / Main. **Gross floor area:** 31.3 m². **Materials:** Tatami mats, polyethylene terephthalate (PET, "polyester"), Tenara polytetrafluoroethylene (PTFE).

Paused for breath

ARCHITECTS: Kengo Kuma & Associates

Tea rooms originally came from a temporary space called a "kakoi", a closed-off room, which is bordered by vertical screens. This breathing architecture is an attempt to approach the original tea room, to confront the non-breathing 20th century concrete architecture. Kuma tries to get to "breathing architecture" via his passive approach to "defeated architecture". "To Breathe" is to have an interaction between environments – at times the architecture becomes small as it holds its breath, and at other times it breathes in deeply to become grander. As the membrane expands and contracts, the room simulates breathing. Tenara was chosen as the membrane material for this project. Unlike conventional membranes, Tenara does not use glass fibers as its base material, making it soft and light. It is highly transparent and achieves intermediacy between reality and the imaginary world, retaining a distinct texture. As a technical note, two membranes with air between them were connected by a polyester string. The joints of the membrane and the strings can be seen as dots.

02

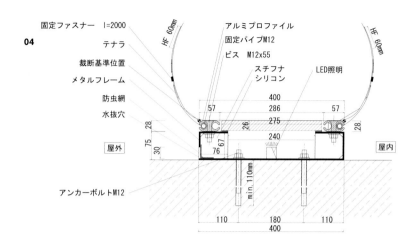

04

固定ファスナー　l=2000
テナラ
裁断基準位置
メタルフレーム
防虫網
水抜穴

HF 60mm

アルミプロファイル
固定パイプM12
ビス　M12x55

スチフナ
シリコン

LED照明

HF 60mm

400
286
57　275　57
28
75　30　67　240
76
26
28

屋外　屋内

アンカーボルトM12

min. 110mm

110　180　110
400

05

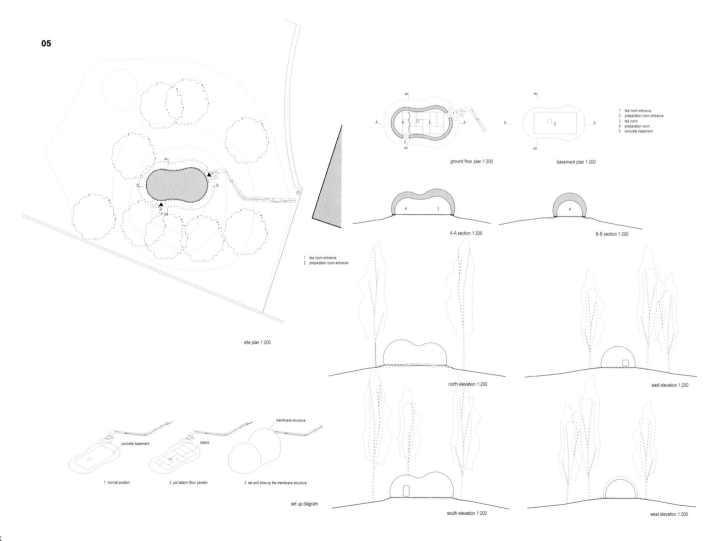

1   tea room entrance
2   preparation room entrance
3   tea room
4   preparation room
5   concrete basement

ground floor plan 1:200

basement plan 1:200

A-A section 1:200

B-B section 1:200

1   tea room entrance
2   preparation room entrance

site plan 1:200

north elevation 1:200

east elevation 1:200

concrete basement

tatami

membrane structure

1. normal position

2. put tatami (floor panels)

3. set and blow up the membrane structure

set up diagram

south elevation 1:200

west elevation 1:200

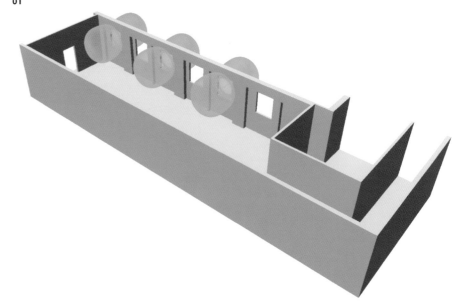

06

**Art project, temporary installation Comfort #3, 2005
Address:** KBB Barcelona, Spain. **Gross floor area:**
220 x 500 cm each. **Materials:** hoses, compressor, foil
made of polyurethane (PU).

Expanding bubbles
ARCHITECTS: Lang / Baumann

Three transparent "sausages", each five meters long and
2.20 meters in diameter have been inserted into the
windows of the art space. By filling the plastic objects
with air, three round bubbles were created in the inner
room, filling it almost completely, and three more outside the façade. Reflections of the outer space are vis-
ibly reflected to the person standing inside and looking
into the bubbles. A third space is formed by the bubbles
themselves, which is interconnecting and pervading, but
is closed in on itself. The artists' work was displayed in
KBB Kültur Büro Barcelona in the context of the "Focus
Switzerland" exhibition with other works from Lang /
Baumann, Fabrice Gygi and Christoph Büchel. The exhibition was curated by Sigismond de Vajay.

01 Isometry **02** View from the roof terrace **03** View from courtyard
04 Detail plastic objects

02

218

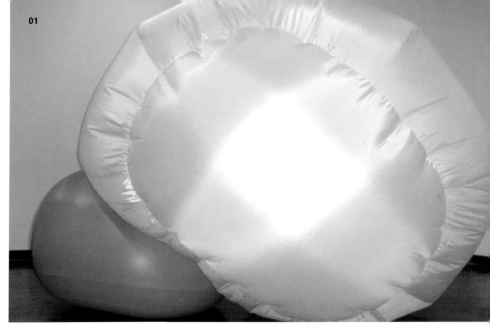

iNSTANT eGO nomadic personal space, 2006
Address: anywhere. **Architects:** Remi Feghali, Adrien Raoul, Hyoungjin Cho. **Client:** Po.D experimental research. **Gross floor area:** 4 m². **Materials:** air pump, motion sensors, computer, video projector, polyvinyl chloride (PVC, "vinyl"), Kevlar© p-phenylene terephtalamides (PPTA, aromatic polyamide, aramids).

The world is my oyster

ARCHITECTS: PoD architecture

iNSTANT eGO is an on-the-go inflatable backpack with a soft LCD skin. It transforms from a folded kit held by zippers on any upper body piece of clothing (jacket, shirt…) into a soft shell that envelops the user once it is unzipped and inflated. The skin consists of a network of pre-shaped inflatable soft PVC tubes supporting a soft LCD fabric. The seat is made of inflatable, high-tolerance PVC. Electronic motion sensors embedded in the structure translate body movements of the occupant into motion in cyberspace. Upon full deployment, the user is entirely "swallowed" by the ephemeral inner chamber, physically plunging through real body movements into virtual cyberspace. The immersive process allows the very real human body to act as a vector inside cyberspace. iNSTANT eGO operates in a continuous metamorphosis from a physical architecture into a virtual one and vice versa. Plastics fulfil the technical requirements of creating a new "intelligent" architecture and are an expression of the boundlessness of architectural creativity.

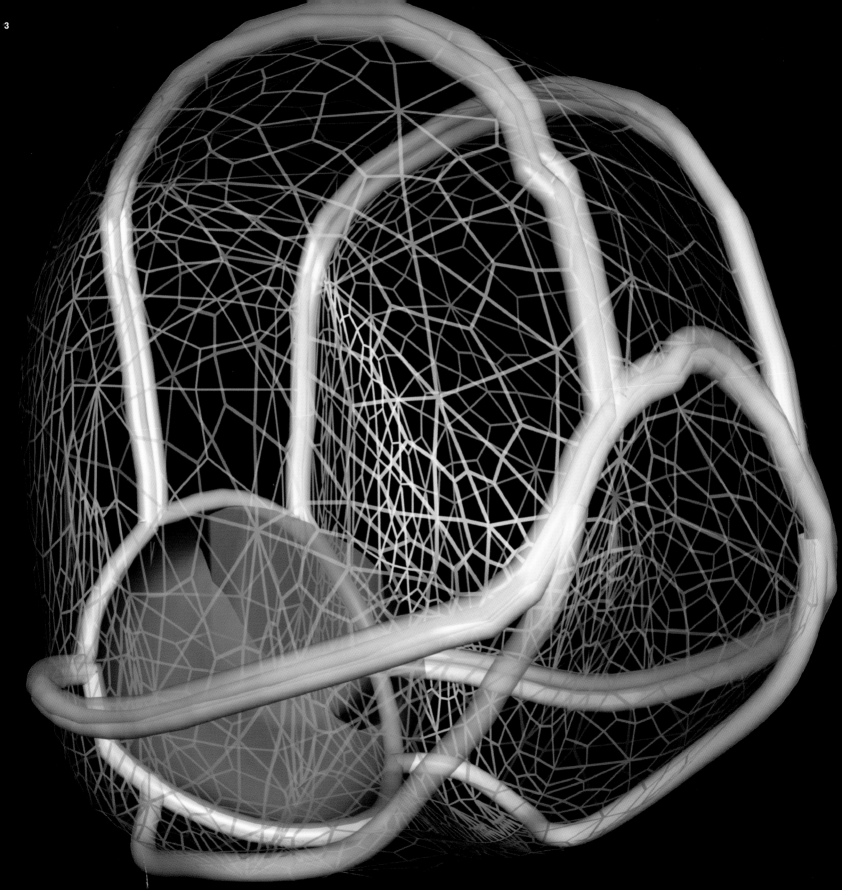

04

05

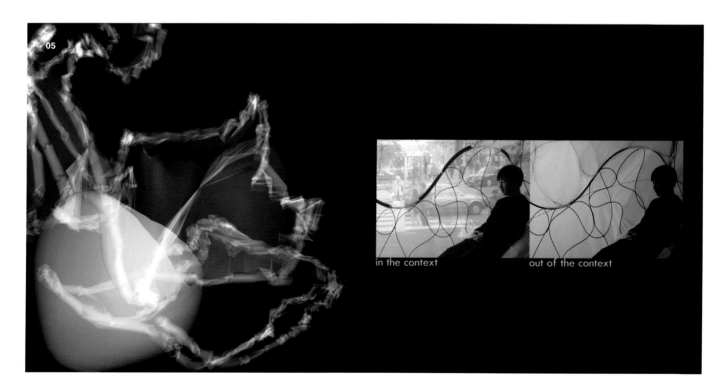

in the context   out of the context

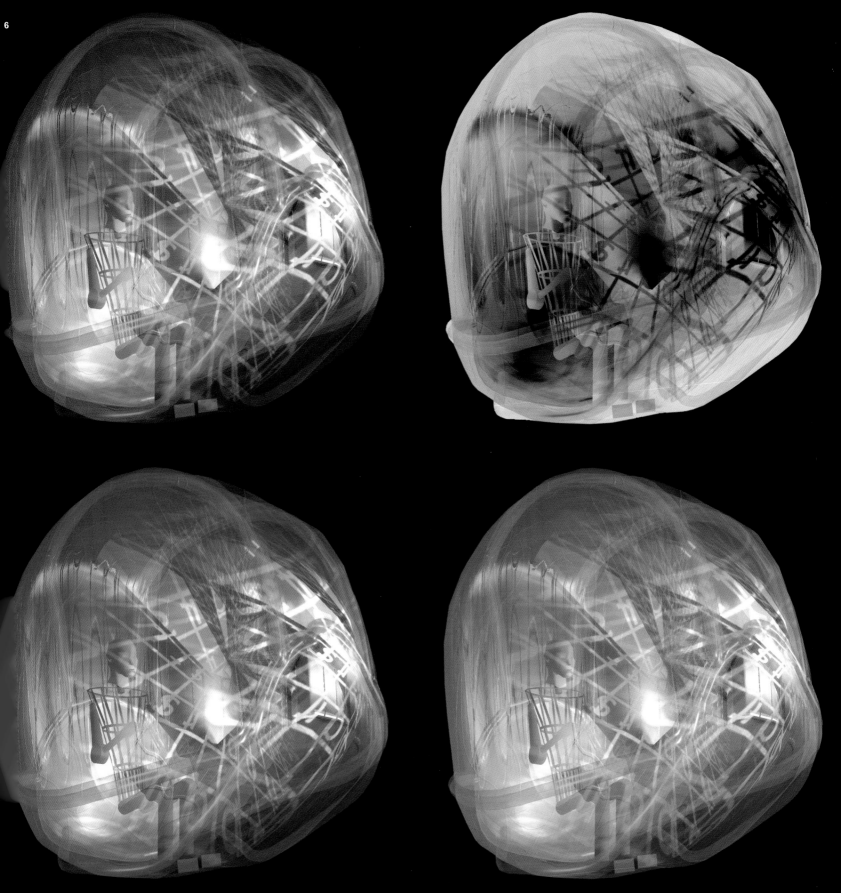

Temporary passage at the International Contemporary Furniture Fair, 2001
Address: Jacob K Javits Convention Center, New York, USA. **Project leader:** Astrid Lipka. **On site installation:** Students of the Integrated Design Curriculum / Parsons School of Design (Gwynne Keathley, director). **Client:** George Little Management / International Contemporary Furniture Fair. **Gross floor area:** 232 m². **Materials:** electrical conduit, springs, red and fluorescent orange polyvinyl chloride (PVC, "vinyl"), polychloroprene (CR, "neoprene") rubber.

Passage

ARCHITECTS: Lyn Rice / OpenOffice

Joining the two locations of the fair taking place in the main Javits Center building and the adjunct North Exhibition Pavilion, the passage is an intimate tubular enclosure that twists in both plan and section to negotiate the transfer between existing access points. The form was not preconceived, but was rather the result of a structural concept of tactical accommodation – a responsive logic that literally worked around existing obstacles. Lyn Rice and Astrid Lipka created 52 sections in a rigorous mapping of the irregular space and its mechanical and structural anomalies. Each idiosyncratic section was morphed with the pure geometry of a simple tube section, resulting in a series of geometrically linked ribs that formed the passage's exoskeleton. This series of outer ribs was deployed in pairs crossed for stability, and they in turn supported dual-color (red and fluorescent orange) interior fabric lining. The inner course enveloped the visitor in multiple layers of supple, vinyl coated polyester mesh, normally used on construction sites and ski runs. The mesh formed a horizontal drape, suspended in tension with thousands of springs clipped to the external system of shaped metal tubing.

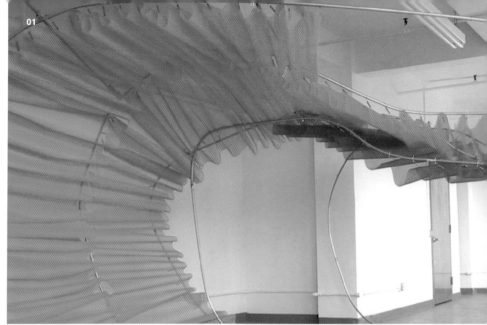

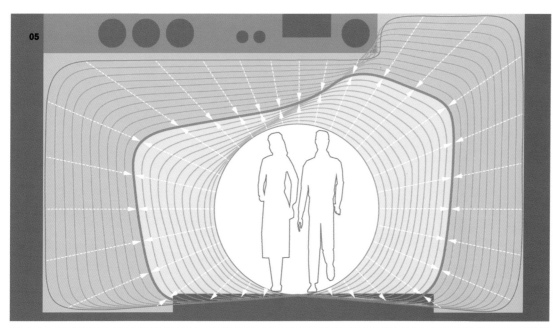

05

01 Construction **02** Detail **03** View through layer of mesh **04** 3D-view **05** Rendered section **06** Rendered floor plan of Javits Center and passage **07** Passage with passengers **08** Passage

06

226

Luminarium Levity II, 2005
Address: itinerant – exhibited in Lithuania, Australia, Spain, Germany, Hungary, France, China, Korea, Eire, Switzerland, Italy, USA, Canada, The Netherlands, Denmark, UK. **Client:** Architects of Air. **Gross floor area:** 1,000 m². **Materials:** air, polyvinyl chloride (PVC, "vinyl")

Bubble wrapped

ARCHITECTS: Alan Parkinson

A luminarium is a monumental installation, which people enter in order to be moved by the beauty of light and color and to experience a sense of wonder. Since 1992, nearly two million visitors from 34 countries across five continents visited the luminaria. They are inspired by pure forms of geometry and nature, Islamic architecture and modern architectural innovators such as Buckminster Fuller and Frei Otto. Since the completion of the first luminarium "Eggopolis" in 1990, all luminaria use some common building blocks such as tunnels, pods and corner domes. These have provided a reliable means of functionally and aesthetically linking the domes. "Arcazaar" (2001) represented a change of approach to the aesthetic of the journey between the domes. Inspired by the modular elements found in Iranian bazaars, a series of small domes linked together replaced the simple cylindrical tunnel. PVC is the material with the optimal properties for this application. It is easy to work with in the workshop and to maintain onsite.

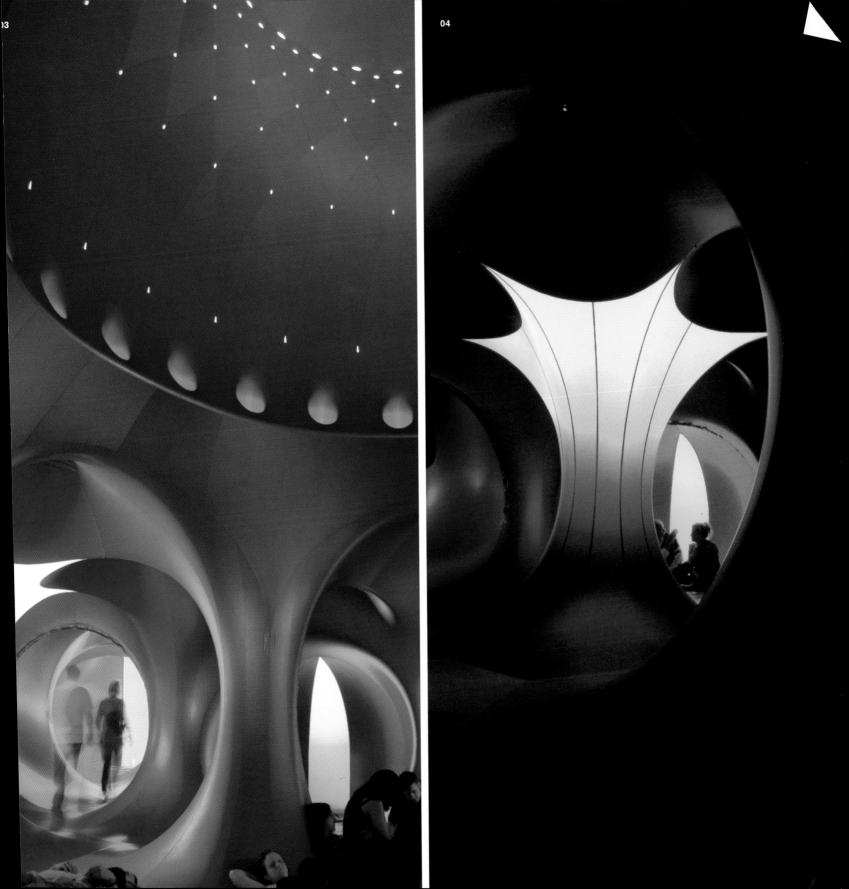

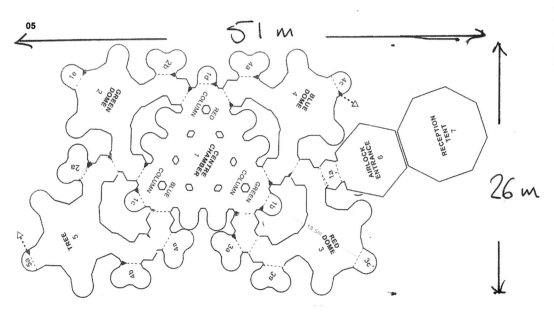

05 ←

51 m

26 m

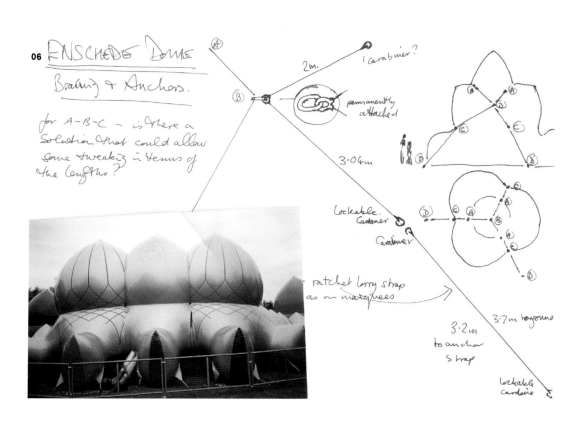

06 ENSCHEDE DOME

Bracing & Anchors.

for A–B–C – is there a solution that could allow some tweaking in terms of the lengths?

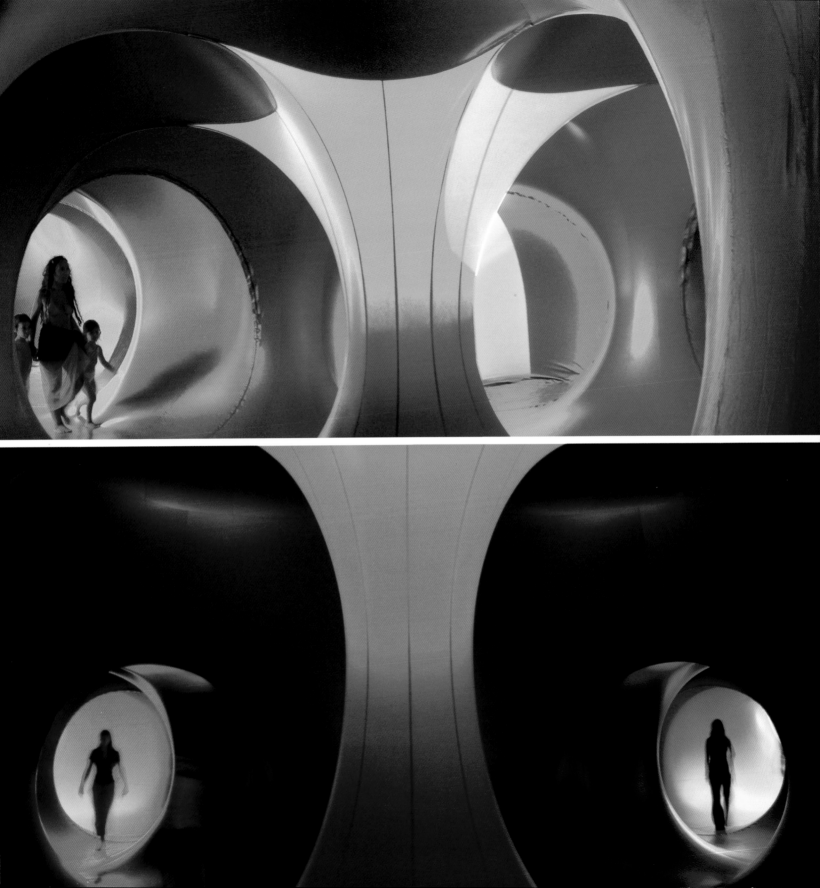

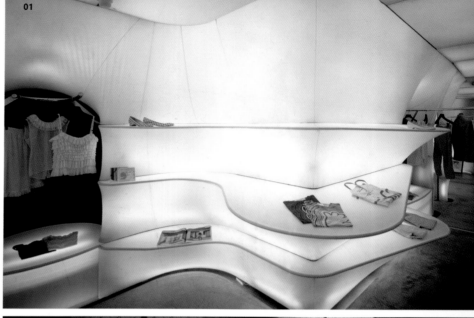

United Bamboo clothing store, 2003
Address: 20–14 Sarugaku-cho, Shibuya-ku, Tokyo 150-0033, Japan. **Client:** JUN. **Gross floor area:** 58 m². **Materials:** steel mesh, steel pipe, faceted glass, fluorescent lights, photo booth camera, computer screen, video projection, iPods & headphones, projection material, polyvinyl chloride (PVC, "vinyl").

Plastic suite

ARCHITECTS: Acconci Studio

An old building has been re-fashioned into a modern clothing shop. A shimmering metal screen camouflages the old façade; glass windows and doors bulge out and push in through the screen. PVC is pulled down to make walls, out to make a counter, pushed and pulled to make shelves. The soft surface draws an analogy to the products being sold. The skin glows due to fluorescent elements embedded within. Non-structural walls have been removed and curving glass alcoves hold racks of hanging clothes outside, against a background of weeds and overgrown shrubbery surrounding the store. If you like how you look in the clothes you might buy, you press a button and your image flashes on a screen on the upper façade, facing the street.

04

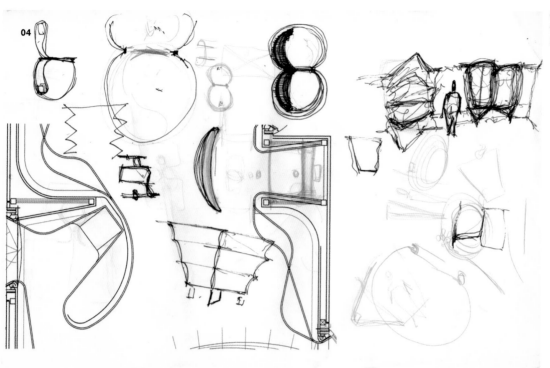

05

06

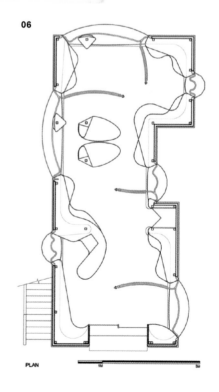

PLAN

United Bottle, 2006
Address: worldwide. **Client:** everyone. **Materials:** polyethylene terephthalate (PET, "polyester").

Genie in a bottle

ARCHITECTS: INSTANT Architects

Whoever has visited developing countries in Asia and Africa certainly knows that plastic bottles are even more common in these regions than in Western Europe or the United States. The architects designed an alternative bottle that can be used as a building material as well. Whenever building material is lacking in a crisis area, bottles can be taken out of the regular recycling circuit and brought there — empty or, if needed, filled with drinking water. The bottles can be filled with sand, earth or liquid or isolating materials like animal hair or feathers and stacked together to form stable structures. Afterwards, they can be returned to the recycling process. These bottles can be also used outside of crisis scenarios as furniture, lamps, garden structures or temporary structures. The bottles' tight stacking also renders them economically viable for soft drink producers, particularly from the point of view of logistics.

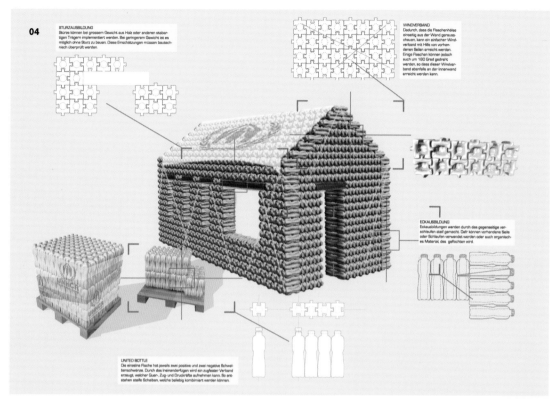

04 STURZAUSBILDUNG
Stürze können bei grossem Gewicht aus Holz oder anderen stabartigen Trägern implementiert werden. Bei geringerem Gewicht ist es möglich ohne Sturz zu bauen. Diese Einschätzungen müssen bautechnisch überprüft werden.

WINDVERBAND
Dadurch, dass die Flaschenhälse einseitig aus der Wand gerausschauen, kann ein einfacher Windverband mit Hilfe von vorhandenen Seilen erreicht werden. Einige Flaschen können jedoch auch um 180 Grad gedreht werden, so dass dieser Windverband ebenfalls an der Innenwand erreicht werden kann.

ECKAUSBILDUNG
Eckausbildungen werden durch das gegenseitige verschlaufen steif gemacht. Dafür können vorhandene Seile oder Schlaufen verwendet werden oder auch organisches Material, das geflochten wird.

UNITED BOTTLE
Die einzelne Flasche hat jeweils zwei positive und zwei negative Schwalbenschwänze. Durch das Ineinanderfügen wird ein zugfester Verband erzeugt, welcher Quer-, Zug- und Druckkräfte aufnehmen kann. So entstehen steife Scheiben, welche beliebig kombiniert werden können.

01 The empty bottles 02 Detail 03 Building made of bottles 04 Sketch of construction 05 The recycling process 06 Bottle filled with sand 07 Interior

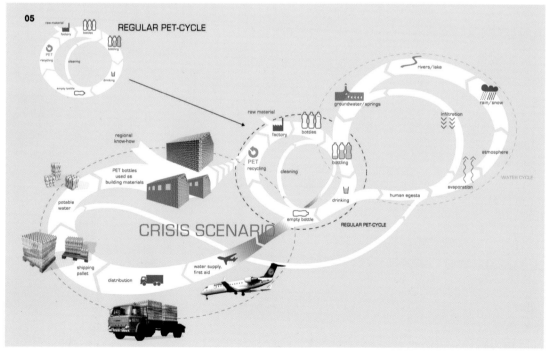

05

REGULAR PET-CYCLE

raw material
factory
bottles
bottling
PET recycling
cleaning
drinking
empty bottle

rivers/lake
groundwater/springs
rain/snow
infiltration
atmosphere
raw material
factory
bottles
PET recycling
cleaning
bottling
drinking
evaporation
human egesta
WATER CYCLE
REGULAR PET-CYCLE

regional know-how
PET bottles used as building materials
potable water
shipping pallet
distribution
water supply, first aid
empty bottle
CRISIS SCENARIO

06

238

Redesign and roofing of Urban-Loritz-Platz, 1999
Address: Urban-Loritz-Platz, Vienna, Austria. **Structural engineers:** Schlaich Bergermann & Partner. **Client:** City of Vienna. **Size:** 2,000 m². **Materials:** steel, glass, membrane, polytetrafluoroethylene (PTFE), polyvinyl chloride (PVC, "vinyl").

Equalizing pulse

ARCHITECTS: Architekten Tillner & Willinger

The Urban-Loritz-Platz is a central traffic junction which, due to its various functions, has been separated into five zones. This development resulted in the plaza no longer being a unified spatial entity, causing lack of orientation and erring traffic routing. The new design should transform the area into a readily-recognizable central auto junction and a link aiding the city's whole operation, repairing its functional deficiencies. A generous roof covers and protects the waiting areas for public transport passengers and walkways leading to them. The roof consists of ten membrane panels. It signals the plaza's new role and enables additional use of this central public space. The plaza surface was redesigned using waiting lounges, kiosks, advertising signs, telephone booths and greenery. The planning of the roof was made more difficult by the fact that only small zones between the underground train tunnel, building extrusions and streetcar rails were available for the roof foundation.

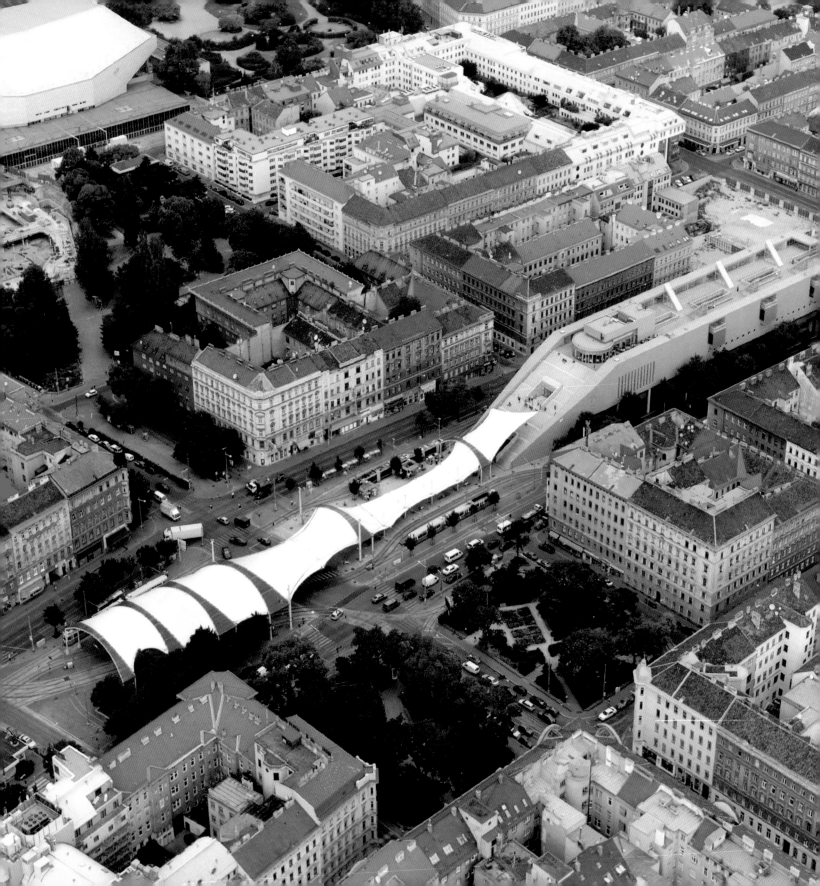

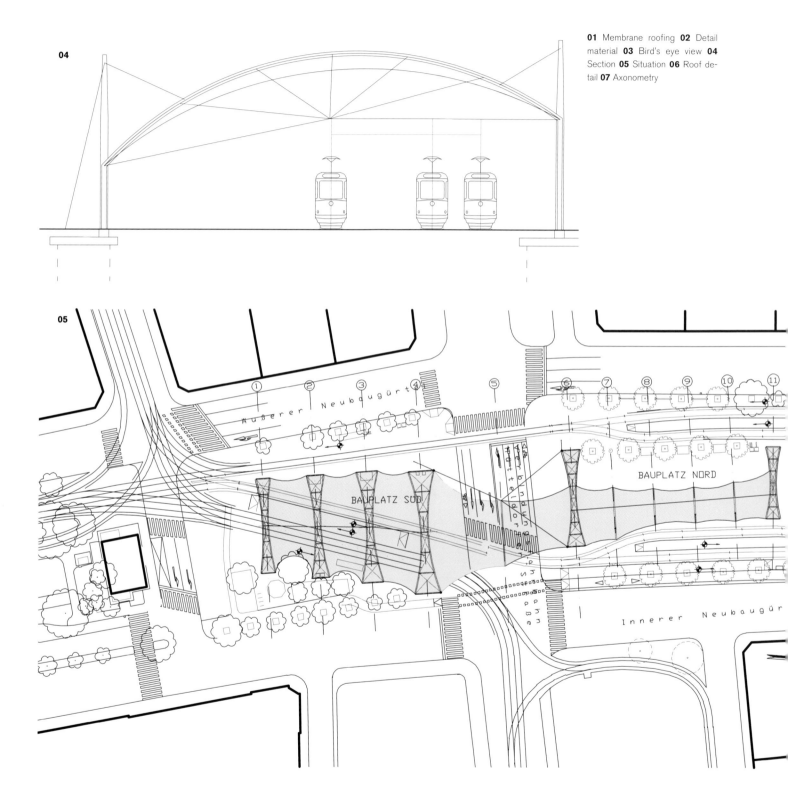

04

05

Äußerer Neubaugürtel

BAUPLATZ SÜD

BAUPLATZ NORD

Innerer Neubaugür

06

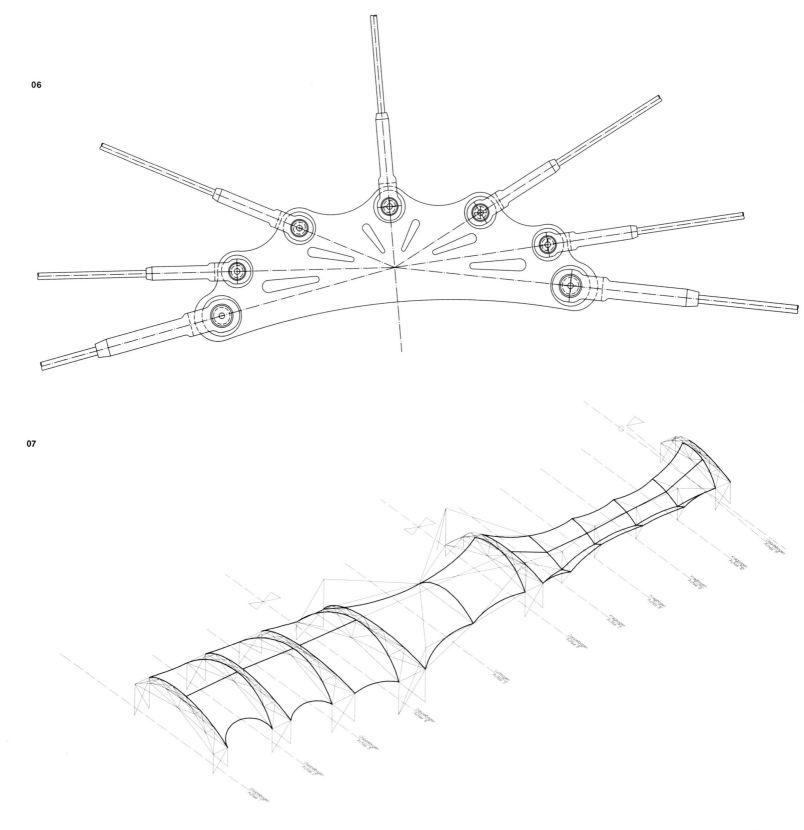

07

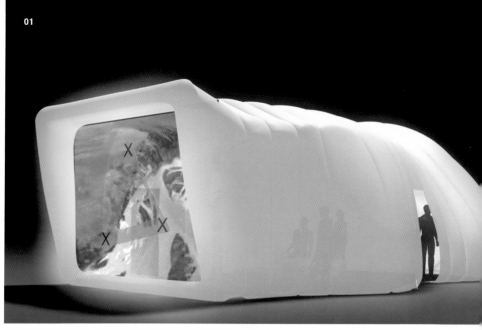

Mobile exhibition pavilion Info Pneu 2 (IP2), 2006
Address: Hagenauer Straße 30, 42107 Wuppertal,
Germany. **Client:** Regionale 2006 GmbH. **Materials:**
canvas made of polyethylene terephthalate (PET, "polyester") covered with polyvinyl chloride (PVC, "vinyl").

Caterpillar with screen

ARCHITECTS: LOBOMOB (Mohamed Fezazi,
Volker Hofmann, Antonio Pinca)

Info Pneu 2 is a temporary mobile exhibition pavilion,
which can be put together in just minutes. Due to its
voluminous design, it changes the perception of public space like a market square, a park or a factory hall
where it is used. The structure's form is free, and is as-
sociated by the visitor with the contents being exhibited.
The outer envelope primarily encases a physical space
which is, secondarily, expanded into a media space using the projector screen. The media presentation element is part of the structure; it multiplies the building
and occupies the city space with an additional dimen-
sion. This synthesis of architectonic unfolding of space
and media communication manifests Info Pneu 2 as a
hybrid space. Coated polyester canvas is used in the
structure. This material fulfils specific requirements that
were crucial for the concept of the building. Ability to
withstand wear and tear, to be hermetic to water and
air, and to conform to basic fire safety regulations were
demanded. The surface gains a degree of individuality
due to its special texture.

05

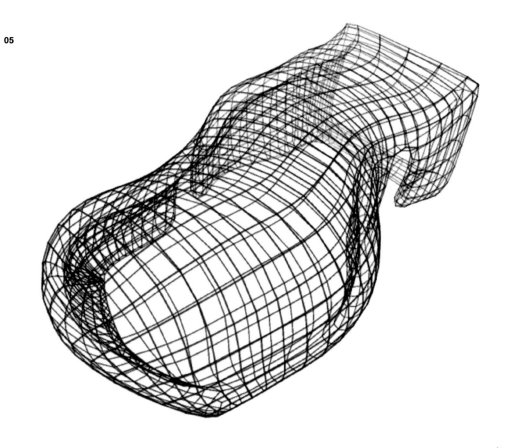

06

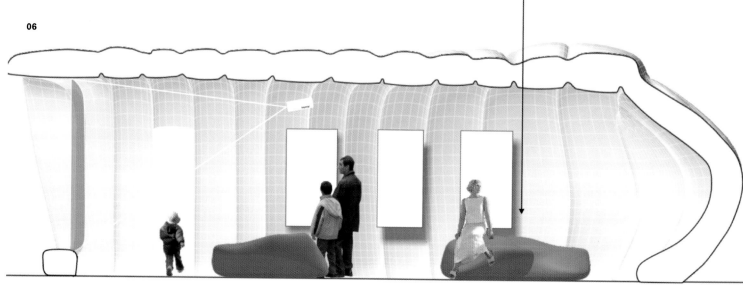

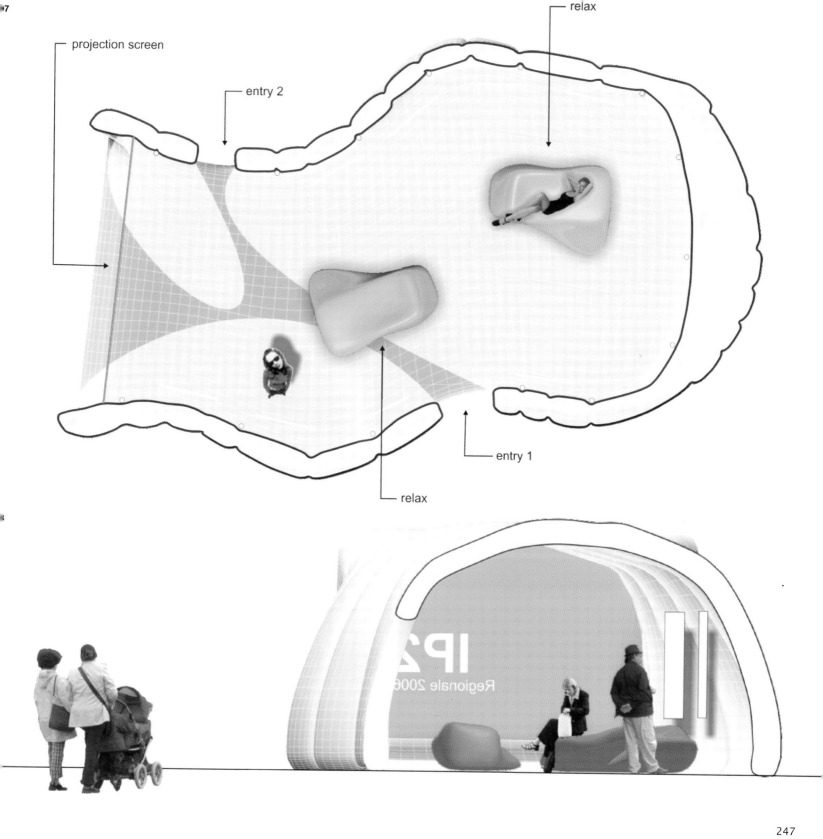

projection screen

entry 2

relax

relax

entry 1

**Ready to plug in "Instant Home – Resident Alien",
2005 / 2007**
Address: anywhere. **Client:** none. **Gross floor area:**
14 m². **Materials:** polyethylene terephthalate (PET,
"polyester"), polyvinyl chloride (PVC, "vinyl")

Out of the box
ARCHITECTS: Valeska Peschke

The Instant Home comes in a box and includes a sofa,
a lamp, a coffee table, a fireplace, a television, a door,
a window, a red-tile roof and a compressor. The most
basic semi-private and public parts of a house as well
as some comfort elements for everyday living are all in-
cluded. Valeska Peschke turned a children's playhouse
into an adult home. With the inflatable home, any public
site can be rededicated to real estate, a private space
for intimacy and creation of identity. The cozy plastic
furniture turns child's play into social commentary about
my-home-is-my-castle-thinking, the ease and comfort
of public space and about childhood. In Los Angeles
and its vicinities as well as in Berlin, Dresden, São Paulo,
Prague and Brussels, the compressor inflated the building in just two minutes, and the artist could observe the
impact of this package on the temporary neighborhood,
inviting passers-by into her home.

01 Instant Home In the desert **02** Ingredients **03** In front of the Semper
opera house, Dresden

RCHITECTS

INDEX

A

Acconci Studio → 232
20 Jay St. Suite 215
Brookyln, NY 11201 (USA)
T +1.7188526591
F +1.7186243178
studio@acconci.com
www.acconci.com

Adria Mobil d.o.o. → 166
Straska cesta 50
8000 Novo mesto (Slovenia)
T +386.7.3937100
F +386.7.3937200
info@adria-mobil.si
www.adria-mobil.com

Angelis Reinhard Architekturbüro
→ 124
Schanzenstraße 21
51063 Cologne (Germany)
T +49.221.612216
F +49.221.612218
mail@angelis-architektur.de

ANA architecten → 94
Tussen de Bogen 38
1013 JB Amsterdam (The Netherlands)
T +31.20.4232949
F +31.20.4232950
mail@ana.nl
www.ana.nl

ARCHTEAM → 74
Namesti Svobody 9
602 00 Brno (Czech Republic)
T +420.5.42213617
F +420.5.42213617
archteam@archteam.cz
www.archteam.cz

B

Bararchitects → 116
Pelgrimstraat 5b
3029 BH Rotterdam (The Netherlands)
T +31.10.4773863
F +31.10.4773863
info@bararchitets.com
www.bararchitets.com

Robert Barnstone → 32
School of Architecture & Construction
Management, PO Box 642220
Pullman, WA 99164-2220 (USA)
T +1.509.335.8196
F +1.509.335.6132
contact@barnstone.com
www.barnstone.com

Becker Architekten → 58
Beethovenstraße 7
87435 Kempten (Germany)
T +49.831.5122000
F +49.831.5122001
kontakt@becker-architekten.net
www.becker-architekten.net

Benthem Crouwel Architekten BV bna
→ 150
Generaal Vetterstraat 61
1059 BT Amsterdam (The Netherlands)
T +31.20.6420105
F +31.20.6465354
bca@benthemcrouwel.nl
www.benthemcrouwel.nl

Randy Brown Architects → 158
1925 N. 120th Street
Omaha, NE 68154 (USA)
T +1.402.5517097
F +1.402.5512033
randy@randybrownarchitects.com
www.randybrownarchitects.com

b&k+ Arno Brandlhuber → 70
Schöneberger Ufer 65
10785 Berlin (Germany)
T +49.171.8676084
mail@brandlhuber.com
www.brandlhuber.com

C

Caramel Architekten ZT GmbH → 84
Schottenfeldgasse 60/36
1070 Vienna (Austria)
T +43.1.5963490
F +43.1.596349020
kha@caramel.at
www.caramel.at

Concrete Architectural Associates → 88
Rozengracht 133 III
1016LV Amsterdam (The Netherlands)
T +31.20.5200200
info@concreteamsterdam.nl
www.concreteamsterdam.nl

Peter Cook (spacelab) → 136

Cottrell & Vermeulen → 98
1b Iliffe Street
London SE17 3LJ (United Kingdom)
T +44.20.77082567
F +44.20.72524742
info@cv-arch.co.uk
www.cv-arch.co.uk

D

deffner voitländer architekten → 90
Gottesackerstraße 21
85221 Dachau (Germany)
T +49.8131.2717.00
F +49.8131.2717.027
werkraum@dv-arc.de
www.dv-arc.de

Dethier & Associés → 62
Rue Fabry 44
4000 Liège (Belgium)
T +32.4.2544850
F +32.4.2544851
architectes@dethier.be
www.dethier.be

Despang Architekten → 154
Am Graswege 5
30169 Hanover (Germany)
T +49.511.882840
F +49.511.887985
info@despangarchitekten.de
www.despangarchitekten.de
www.armstrong.de

Deutsche Bundesstiftung Umwelt DBU
→ 54
An der Bornau 2
49090 Osnabrück (Germany)
T +49.541.96330
F +49.541.9633190
www.dbu.de

Dil en Bonazzi Architecten → 130
Groenhoedenveem 16
1019 BL Amsterdam (The Netherlands)
T +39.20.3205996
F +39.20.3205989
info@dilbonazzi.nl
www.dilbonazzi.nl

Hugo Dworzak → 174
Pestalozziweg 7
6890 Lustenau (Austria)
T +43.5577.20706
F +43.5577.2070615
office@hugodworzak.at
www.austria-architects.com/hugo.dworzak

F

Fischer Art AG Architekturstudio → 46
Westquai 39
4003 Basel (Switzerland)
T + 41.61.272.72.58
architekten@fischerart.ch
www.fischerart.ch

**FORMORF
(Marco Hemmerling, Markus Holzbach)**
→ 210
Wormser Straße 37 – Gartenhaus
50677 Cologne (Germany)
T +49.171.2082089
info@formorf.com
www.formorf.com

Foster + Partners → 78, 188
Riverside, 22 Hester Road
London SW11 4AN (United Kingdom)
T +44.20.77380455
F +44.20.77381107
press@fosterandpartners.com
www.fosterandpartners.com

Colin Fournier (spacelab) → 136

Franken-Architekten → 146
Niddastraße 84
60329 Frankfurt / Main (Germany)
T +49.69.2972830
F +49.69.29728329
office@franken-architekten.de
www.franken-architekten.de

John Friedman Alice Kimm Architects
→ 66
701 East Third Street, Suite 300
Los Angeles, CA 90013 (USA)
T +1.213.2534740
F +1.213.2534760
info@jfak.net
www.jfak.net

Massimiliano Fuksas architetto → 120
Piazza del Monte di Pietà, 30
00186 Rome (Italy)
T +39.06.68807871
F+ 39.06.68807872
office@fuksas.it
www. fuksas.it

G

Fritz Gampe → 130
Milow 67
17337 Uckerland (Germany)
T +49.39753.26651
M +49.171.8228581
Fritz.Gampe@gmx.net

graciastudio → 26
6151 Progressive Ave. Suite 200
San Diego, CA 92154 (USA)
T +1.619.7957864
F +1.619.2693103
info@graciastudio.com
www.graciastudio.com

Graft, Gesellschaft von Architekten mbH
→ 198
Heidestraße 50
10557 Berlin (Germany)
T +49.30.24047985
F +49.30.24047987
berlin@graftlab.com
www.graftlab.com

Gruber + Popp Architekten BDA → 106
Am Spreebord 5
10589 Berlin (Gemany)
T +49.30.6880966
F +49.30.68809666
architekten@gruberpopp.de
www.gruberpopp.de

H

Zaha Hadid Architects → 194
Studio 9, 10 Bowling Green Lane
London EC1R 0BQ (United Kingdom)
T +44.20.72535147
F +44.20.72518322
mail@zaha-hadid.com
www.zaha-hadid.com

I

INSTANT Architects → 236
Weinbergstrasse 135
8006 Zurich (Switzerland)
T +41.79.6786883
info@instant-arch.net
www.instant-arch.net

J

JAKOB + MACFARLANE → 186
13–15 Rue des petites ecuries
75010 Paris (France)
T +33.1.44790572
F +33.1.48009793
jakmak@club-internet.fr
www.jakobmacfarlane.com

Johnsen Schmaling Architects
→ 42
1699 N. Astor Street
Milwaukee, WI 53202 (USA)
T +1.414.2879000
F +1.414.2879025
info@johnsenschmaling.com
www.johnsenschmaling.com

K

Reiner Kliebhan → 58
reiner.kliebhan@t-online.de

Kengo Kuma & Associates
→ 10, 102, 214
2-24-8 Minami Aoyama, Minato-ku
Tokyo, 107.0062 (Japan)
T +81.3.3401.7721
F +81.3.3401.7778
kuma@ba2.so-net.ne.jp
www.kkaa.co.jp

Ivan Kroupa architekti → 40
Ricanska 7
101 00 Prague 10 – Vinohrady
(Czech Republic)
T +420.2.44460103
ivankroupa@ivankroupa.cz
www.ivankroupa.cz

kuntz+manz architekten → 54
Beethovenstraße 5
97080 Würzburg (Germany)
T +49.931.797250
F +49.931.7972520
info@kuntzundmanz.de
www.kuntzundmanz.de

L

Lang / Baumann → 218
Lyssachstrasse 112
3400 Burgdorf (Switzerland)
T +41.34.4220424
F +41.344230617
lb@langbaumann.com
www. langbaumann.com

Atelier Van Lieshout → 200
Keilestraat 43E
3029 BP Rotterdam (The Netherlands)
T +31.10.2440971
F +31.10.2440972
info@ateliervanlieshout.com
www.ateliervanlieshout.com

LOBOMOB → 244
Hagenauer Straße 30
42107 Wuppertal (Germany)
T +49.202.3719362
F +49.202.3719359
info@lobomob.de
www.lobomob.de

LTL Architects → 30
227 West 29th Street, 7th Fl.
New York, NY 10001 (USA)
T +1.221.5055955
F +1.221.5051648
office@ltlarchitects.com
www.ltlarchitects.com

Greg Lynn Form → 204
1817 Lincoln Boulevard
Venice, CA 90291 (USA)
T +1.310.8212629
F +1.310.8219729
node@glform.com
www.glform.com

M

Makoto Sei Watanabe → 110
1-23-30-2806, Azumabashi, Sumida-ku
Tokyo 130-0001 (Japan)
F +81.3.38293837
www.makoto-architect.com
msw@makoto-architect.com

Doriana Mandrelli → 120

Dorte Mandrup Arkitekter → 70
Nørrebrodgade 66d
2200 Copenhagen N (Denmark)
T +45.33937350
F +45.33935360
info@dortemandrup.dk
www.dortemandrup.dk

Carlos Martinez Architekten AG
→ 162, 202
Sonnenstrasse 8b
9443 Widnau (Switzerland)
T +41.71.7279955
F +41.71.7279944
cam@carlosmartinez.ch
www.carlosmartinez.ch

Nina Mihovec
c/o WilsonicDesign → 166
Sp. Senica 10b
1215 Medvode (Slovenia)
T +386.1.3611278
F +386.1.3613095
nina.mihovec@wilsonicdesign.com
www.wilsonicdesign.com

N

Niemann Architekten → 114
Klopstockplatz 9
22765 Hamburg (Germany)
T +49.40.856763
F +49.40.856764
post@niemann-architekten.de
www.niemann-architekten.de

NIO Architecten → 178
Schiedamse Vest 95a
3012 BG Rotterdam (The Netherlands)
T +31.10.4122318
F +31.10.4126075
nio@nio.nl
www.nio.nl

NL Architects → 182
Van Hallstraat 294
1051 HM Amsterdam (The Netherlands)
T +31.20.6207323
F +31.20.6386192
office@nlarchitects.nl
www.nlarchitects.nl

NOX / Lars Spuybroek → 144
Postbox 620
3000 AP Rotterdam (The Netherlands)
T +31.10.4772853
F +31.10.4772853
info@noxarch.com
www.noxarch.com

NTT International b.v. (i.o.) →130
Amsterdam (The Netherlands)
f.gampe@go-ntt.com
www.go-ntt.com

O

ONL [Oosterhuis_Lénárd] →170
Essenburgsingel 94c
3022 EG Rotterdam (The Netherlands)
T +31.10.2447039
F +31.10.2447041
info@oosterhuis.nl
www.oosterhuis.nl

Picture Credits

All other pictures were made available by the architects

Cover
front side: Richard Osborn
back side: NOX / Lars Spuybroek (l.)
Craig Kuhner (r.)